To Theresa

The Eleventh Hour
Can't Last Forever

Alison Johnson

The Eleventh Hour
Can't Last Forever

Alison Johnson

Cumberland Press
Brunswick, Maine

ISBN 13: 978-0-9675619-2-9

ISBN 10: 0-9675619-2-2

Printed in the United States of America

This is a true story; nothing has been added or embellished. I have only changed the names of a few people not central to the main action and the first names of my daughters to afford them a degree of privacy. I wrote this family memoir in 1984-85 but delayed publishing it while my brothers were still alive.

CHAPTER ONE

Two tons of silver and gold coins, hundreds of thousands of nickels, dimes, quarters, and gold pieces. They were under our beds, in the kitchen cupboards, up in the attics, in the bottom of dresser drawers, in holes in the ground. My father was obsessed with gathering up these coins and hiding them away in any likely spot in the houses and garages and store buildings he owned in our tiny town on the mid-Western prairie. Nothing could shake his belief that the total collapse of the American economy and government was just around the corner, a collapse that would bring anarchy and rioting in the streets. With this shadow of Armageddon always hanging over him, Dad believed that he could save his family from disaster only by collecting as much gold and silver as he could lay his hands on.

This fear of a future calamity that might leave his family penniless so dominated Dad's thoughts that he failed to see how his blind absorption in amassing wealth created family problems that would lead to his oldest son's hopeless alcoholism and his wife's mental collapse. My sister grew up so insecure that she eventually turned to the stars for answers to the frustrations of her life, immersing herself in the study of astrology. In the fairy tale, King Midas's daughter was miraculously restored to life after she had been turned to stone by her father's desire for gold, but Dad's destructive influence on his family could not be so easily reversed.

Our family home was in the small town of Palisade on the Nebraska prairie. Palisade lay in a flat river valley, and the hills that surrounded it on all sides cut off any extended view of a world beyond. Since rainfall in southwestern Nebraska was meager, the countryside yielded only a few scattered cottonwood trees clinging to the banks of the river or the tiny creeks trickling into it. The only large plants to survive on the open prairie were sunflowers and tall weeds that dried up in the autumn into prickly golden tumbleweeds that rolled restlessly over the fields, driven by the relentless winds sweeping across the plains.

When I was a child, Palisade had a population of 799. Everyone vaguely thought it should have been possible to come up with one more living soul to push us to the more impressive figure of 800, but 799 it was, and from this peak the population declined to 350 in only a few decades. Even the surrounding counties were sparsely populated. Palisade lay halfway between Denver and Lincoln, 250 miles from each–about as far as one could get from civilization in the United States. From the hills encircling the town, one could look for miles in any direction and see only an occasional farmhouse with its straggly windbreak of Russian olive trees, planted because they were one of the few trees that would survive wind and drought.

Grandfather Krotter came to Palisade in 1894 to manage a lumber-yard when the town was only a pioneer settlement of a dozen buildings. Before long he owned the yard, and within a decade he had become a highly successful businessman, with lumberyards, grain elevators, and huge ranches scattered over four counties. Although his formal educa-tion was limited, he had a brilliant mind and an unusual ability to handle the practical problems of creating businesses on the empty Nebraska prairie. On one occasion, impatient with the slow progress of two surveyors he had hired, he spent an afternoon watching how they practiced their trade. The next day he fired them, bought himself the necessary equipment, and henceforth did all of his own surveying. He taught himself trigonometry and studied books on electricity and physics so that he could build a hydroelectric plant on a nearby river to provide Palisade with electricity. When he died of a heart attack in 1936, he left his heirs a chain of eight lumberyards, four grain elevators, two hardware stores, and fourteen thousand acres of Nebraska farm land. The lead story in the newspaper of a nearby town stated: "There was perhaps no greater amount of energy, ambition, business acumen, perseverance, honor and integrity involved in the make up of any one citizen in the state than did Mr. Krotter possess."

My grandfather wanted, however, to create not only a business empire, but also a Krotter dynasty to enjoy and extend the fruits of his genius. In one of the towns where he ran a lumberyard, he met a young music teacher with a similar German immigrant background. After a brief courtship, they were married in 1899. My grandmother typified the position of a woman in the Victorian age. A strong-willed German father had dominated her youth, and she married a man who controlled half the county. In my grandparents' wedding photograph, their characters and personalities seem unmistakable, with his handsome face beaming success and confidence, while her beautiful eyes disclose timidity and fearfulness.

Their two sons, Dean and Chauncey, couldn't have been more different from each other. The younger son, Chauncey, enjoyed working with people and was also at ease running farm machinery or herding cattle on horseback. It was natural that he eventually handled all the Krotter ranch interests. By contrast, my father, Dean, was shy and introverted, a sensitive, unhappy child who immersed himself in books and remained a loner. He was tall but thin and uncoordinated, so he was not readily accepted by the other boys in town, whose lives revolved around sports and games. And of course the underlying resentments of various townspeople about the amount of financial control my grandfather wielded over the town were all too easily picked up by their children. Dad was certainly an easier target than his father or brother. Perhaps it was because he felt rejected by other children that Dad tried especially hard to please his father, for whom he felt an overwhelming love and admiration. Even as a child he never doubted that he would follow in his father's footsteps and work in the family business. Because Grandfather Krotter needed someone to run his power company, Dad spent a year doggedly studying electricity at a technical institute in Washington, D.C., although he had no interest in the subject. Even long after my grandfather's death, his presence and authority still seemed to radiate inescapably down upon Dad from his picture hanging above the office desk.

Like Grandfather Krotter, Dad believed strongly in the concept of dynasty. After graduating from the University of Nebraska with a degree in business administration and settling into his father's business, he set about choosing a wife. A study of eugenics had convinced him that he should marry a very intelligent woman in order to have smart children. As luck would have it, as a member of the Palisade school board, he went to the University of Nebraska in Lincoln to hire a high school English teacher and interviewed my future mother, Audrey Musick, a top graduate of the university. Impressed by her academic record, Dad gave her the job as English teacher and within two years chose her to fill the position of his wife.

Mom was born on a farm near Edgar, Nebraska, in 1905. When she was six years old, her father decided to give up farming and bought a general store in Summerfield, Kansas, only sixty miles south of Lincoln, Nebraska. Mom's parents provided her with a happy home and child-hood, marred only as the economic hardships of the 1920s overtook small country towns. Since my grandfather was forced to close his store shortly before my mother wanted to start college, he was able to give her little help. Despite her difficult financial position, Mom was deter-mined to get a college degree at the University of Nebraska. She achieved this goal by working part-time in a department store in Lincoln while she attended classes and by interrupting her studies for a couple of years to teach in a high school in Summerfield. Forced to budget her money very carefully during her college years, she often made a meager meal of a bowl of rice and a piece of fruit in the student cafeteria. Thirty years later she could still remember the exact price of each item.

Countless details of my mother's life came to me over the years through family stories she or her sister, Thelma, told me. Caught in a frustrating marriage, Mom relived in conversations with us children how it had all come about, perhaps thereby trying to understand for herself the mistakes she so regretted.

Mom had often told me that it was financial necessity that brought her to Palisade to teach, since she was helping to support her parents and put her brother through dental school. Her university degree had been in journalism, but good newspaper jobs were difficult to obtain. With her heavy financial burdens, she had little choice but to settle for a teaching job.

When Dad started courting Mom, she readily accepted his invitations to dinner and a concert or movie. He was not only the son of the leading citizen of the county, but he was also tall, good-looking, and intellectual. She never suspected that Dad didn't really enjoy social occasions but was just going through a ritual of courtship. Aunt Thelma later told me a revealing story about Dad's first visit to their home. When Dad spent more time reading than getting acquainted with my mother's family, Aunt Thelma complained to her mother, "Why does Audrey want to marry him? He's always got his nose in a book." Since Mom loved to read too, she thought that was an interest they shared. Only later did she realize the extent to which Dad would withdraw from the world around him to give all his attention to financial and political publications. When I was a child and we had guests in our home for an evening, he would frequently escape to an adjoining room to read while the rest of us entertained them.

When Dad proposed to Mom in 1932, she faced a difficult decision. At the height of the Depression, he offered her wealth and status, and she had no way of foreseeing that the money she thought would ease her path through life would become a curse. If she hadn't married him, she would have had to continue teaching to support herself and help her family. It wasn't a profession she enjoyed, but there were few other jobs available during those years. Although I know that Mom had a great respect for Dad and thought he was a fine person, I find it hard to believe she was in love with him. He had many traits that worried her, but in her youthful optimism she hoped to change his behavior once they were married. One incident prior to their wedding epitomized all too clearly Dad's odd ideas. He suggested to Mom that one of his former girlfriends, who was a home-economics teacher, could pick out their wedding china. Mom was highly offended by this insensitive sugges-tion, but she failed to realize the extent to which Dad's blindness about human relations would make him a difficult husband.

It was easy for Mom to be overwhelmed by the offer of a honeymoon in Europe that accompanied Dad's proposal. Perhaps without fully realizing it, she let this prospect unduly influence her decision to marry him. Europe was indeed a dream come true for her, but the trip had disquieting undertones. Now that he had won her, Dad began to retreat back into his books. On shipboard he left his beautiful wife alone so often that another young man attempted to become friendly with her and other passengers started raising their eyebrows. On another occasion, Mom was walking around the grounds of an English castle when a man asked if he could join her. She dismissed him by saying, "That's my husband over there behind the cannon, reading a book." Mom was eager to go out in the evenings, but she had no choice but to walk the streets of foreign cities alone, while Dad read at their hotel.

When they returned to Nebraska, Mom was unhappy to find that Dad would no longer give up evenings for dinner parties, as he had willingly done during their courtship. At that time, there was an active social group of young married couples in town that Mom wanted very much to be a part of, but Dad preferred to spend his evenings working at the office or reading an investment book at home. Within a few months of their return from Europe, however, Mom became pregnant, and the pleasure she felt at the prospect of having a baby served to counterbalance her growing dismay at my father's shortcomings. The letters she wrote to her mother after the birth of my brother Kent in 1933 are full of the joy of new motherhood.

An incident Mom used to tell us about Kent's birth indicated all too clearly the problems in her relationship with Dad. It was a long and difficult birth, and when she woke up from anesthesia after the ordeal, she hoped to see Dad. She was very disappointed to learn, however, that he had already left the hospital to go home to Palisade to share with his parents the news that he had a new son.

Mom liked Grandfather Krotter very much because he had a pleasant, sociable personality. Grandmother Krotter, however, was a repressed woman with many eccentric habits. One year she read an article expounding the theory that it was healthy to walk backwards. For several weeks she had someone drive her out to the country every day so that she could walk backwards into town. When Mom first visited in the Krotter home, she was appalled to see that Grandmother Krotter's idea of a family dinner was to be in constant motion between the kitchen and the dining room table, anticipating every desire of her husband and two sons. No sacrifice was too great for her to make for the men in her family. Her comments about Dad usually included the words "poor Dean," and she clearly viewed my mother as a reinforcement in the ranks dedicated to smoothing his path through life.

Mom found it particularly difficult to celebrate Christmas with the Krotters because they did little to observe the holiday and didn't even bother to put up a tree. The second Christmas after her marriage, she gave up on the Krotters and took the train home with her seven-week-old baby to spend Christmas with her own family, who despite their limited means at least knew how to enjoy life.

From Aunt Thelma, I learned that Mom considered the possibility of divorce early in her marriage. She was basically a conventional person, however, and divorce was a highly unusual step at that time. I can remember many conversations in which Mom or other women in the family would refer to someone as a "divorced woman" in a tone of voice that subtly conveyed the message that these people lived on the fringes of society. The responsibility of a new baby also greatly complicated

Mom's situation, but this was only one of her problems. Dad was sending money to help support my grandparents and to put my uncle through dental school. If Mom had left him, this support would have been lost to her family. To make matters worse, she would have also felt a great moral obligation to repay the money Dad had already expended on them. In the depths of the Depression, that must have seemed a formidable undertaking.

The most difficult aspect of Mom's dilemma, however, was that Dad was basically well meaning and believed himself to be a good and considerate husband. Mom was a very kind person, and her knowledge of how much she would hurt Dad if she left him acted as a strong restraint against her desire to escape. So it was that in the mid-1930s she found herself trapped and settled down for life to make the best of it, putting all her vitality and love into raising a family.

Three more children were eventually born to my parents: my sister Diane in 1936, myself in 1939, and my brother Mark in 1947. By the time I arrived, my family was living on a ninety-acre farm adjoining Palisade, our house separated from the edge of town only by a large cornfield. The town itself was neatly laid out, with all the businesses lining two or three blocks of Main Street and residential areas spreading for four or five blocks on either side. The Krotter family home in the center of Palisade, then occupied only by my grandmother, was an unusually large and impressive structure for a small prairie town. The house and yard occupied a full quarter of a square block shaded by half a dozen beautiful old elm trees. Eight large columns surrounded the porch in a rural Nebraska version of Grecian grandeur.

Family patterns were clearly established by the time I appeared on the scene. After Grandfather Krotter died in 1936, my father ran the lumberyards and Uncle Chauncey managed the Palisade farm and the ranches. Ten years later my uncle died, leaving Dad burdened with even more responsibility.

By the late 1940s, the conditions that had enabled my grandfather to accumulate a fortune in two decades were gone forever. Now many families owned a car and could drive thirty miles to the larger towns to shop. When this new mobility led to depressed conditions in the smaller towns in the late 1950s and early 1960s, Dad was forced to close one after another of his lumberyards and elevators. It must have been a wrenching experience for him to watch the continuous erosion of the business empire created by the father he had worshiped. When I was a child, our town boasted five groceries, five filling stations, and other assorted businesses on a busy Main Street. It was hard to find a place to park on Saturday night, when the stores were open and the farmers all came into town to do their weekly shopping. Now abandoned stores line the business district, their streaked and dusty windows offering only a dim view of empty and faded interiors, where shelves once laden with merchandise are now barren of anything but a few dead flies. It is not unusual to see two drivers stop their cars in the middle of the deserted Main Street to carry on a leisurely conversation before continuing on their way.

Perhaps it was because he sensed he was fighting a losing battle that Dad worked constantly, often returning to the office after dinner in the evening. Saturday was always a regular work day, and he usually worked Sundays too. The term "workaholic" had not yet been coined, but it describes Dad perfectly. He always complained when his store managers went fishing on Sunday because he wished them to be near the phone in case a customer ran out of paint.

I remember vividly an unusual Sunday afternoon when Dad took us children out to the country to play. It made a strong impression upon me because he so rarely found time to spend with us. On that occasion, we ended up crawling through some rather dangerous tunnels in a dirt cliff while Dad was totally absorbed in a book.

Although Dad spent almost no time with us, he was proud of us and loved us very much. Unfortunately, he could show his affection only by accumulating as much money as possible for us as protection against some disaster lurking in the future. Money, however, was always a mixed blessing for our family. It gave us many advantages, but it also isolated us and set us apart within that little town where some of the children we played with didn't even have indoor plumbing. No one else in Palisade came close to having as much money as we had, and as children we found our family's wealth a source of constant embarrassment. One year Dad bought a fourth car, much to my chagrin. I lived in dread of the occasions when all four cars happened to be parked outside at once because in my childish naïveté, I hoped that people might not have noticed how many we had. Our financial position caused problems for Kent also; older boys would taunt him, saying his family kept shoe boxes full of money in the closets. At that time those were only adolescent gibes, and little did any of us realize that the taunts were prophetic.

CHAPTER TWO

When I was only two years old, my maternal grandparents moved into a small house on our farm. Their place quickly became my second home, and a deep bond grew between my grandfather and me because he adored little children. Before long, he had virtually assumed the role of father in my life.

Grandfather Musick looked after various chores on the farm; at that time we still raised chickens and had a couple of horses. Mom always joked that although Dad owned eight lumberyards, she had never seen him drive a nail. Grandfather did all the carpentry jobs around the farm and began teaching me to handle a hammer when I could barely lift it. When there was no work to be done, we spent hours playing rummy.

Although Grandfather was very intelligent, his interests were not particularly intellectual. This may have been because he had missed his chance for an education. The day before his intended departure for college, his family's farm was hit by a hail storm. The next morning his father took him out to survey the ruined corn crop and said, "There's your college education." But despite this early disappointment, Grandfather's outlook on life remained positive; he enjoyed people and everyone liked him. Even as a child I sensed the sharp contrast between my father's withdrawal into a world of abstractions and my grandfather's enthusiastic enjoyment of life. In my childhood memories of Dad, I usually see him engrossed in reading a financial chart. When I think of Grandfather Musick, however, I often remember him singing "McNamara's Band" with great gusto as he tapped his foot.

Colorful Nebraska expressions enlivened Grandfather's speech. When my brother Kent would offer some rather abstract opinion, Grandfather would bring him back to earth with the comment, "You know about as much about that as a hog knows about a holiday." Or if we girls were overly concerned about some flaw in our apparel, he would say, "It'll never be seen from a galloping horse."

Grandfather had a natural talent for music and played many different instruments by ear. In his youth he had fiddled for country dances in Nebraska. Although his fingers had with age become rather stiff, he would occasionally play for us when we begged him to do so. Our special delight was to have him sit down at his old piano to play and sing "The Old Grey Mare, She Ain't What She Used to Be," using only the black keys. Grandmother Musick was a semi-invalid, having broken her back several years before, but she exerted a quiet and kind influence on those around her from the corner of the couch where she usually sat sewing. As she worked, she entertained me with story after story from her early memories of pioneer days in Illinois and Nebraska. I don't think she fully realized her dramatic powers, and her tales of children overtaken by tornadoes on the Nebraska prairie left me terror-stricken whenever the sky darkened and the wind rose. One of my favorite stories was about her childhood dismay when the daughter of immigrant neighbors proudly invited her to come over to their farmhouse for a special treat of blood pudding.

On warm evenings I would sit with my grandparents on their front porch. Nebraska sunsets, made glorious by the heavy dust content of the prairie air, seemed a recompense for everything else nature had denied the state. Together we looked out over the cornfields, watching the sun sink down and the clouds float slowly across a wide sky brilliant with rose and gold tints. My grandparents would talk quietly, and from their stories I got a glimpse of what farm life was like on the frontier of the 1880s. There was a special quality of companionship and repose in those evenings that would remain in my memory long after my grandparents had died.

The tranquility of their home was a relief for me from the underlying tension that was always present between my parents, whose differing attitudes toward life caused frequent verbal clashes. When I was about ten years old, I lived in fear of Dad and Mom getting a divorce, although I realize now that there was no question of their separating at that particular time.

An incident that seared itself into my memory occurred one day when Mom was driving the car to town. As we approached the intersection of our gravel road with the highway, Dad started giving Mom advice about approaching traffic. He could be very irritating with his constant suggestions, and on this occasion Mom angrily slammed on the brakes. Three-year-old Mark flew into the windshield with a sickening thud and started to cry. The argument continued on the other side of the highway, and suddenly Mom slammed on the brakes a second time. Once again Mark crashed into the windshield, and I felt as if I were hitting it with him.

Although Mom and Dad's arguments were rarely this extreme, their frequency left us all feeling insecure. Diane seemed to be particularly affected. Throughout her troubled childhood, she was very moody and cried frequently. At night she was so terrified that Mom often had to spend hours trying to get her to fall asleep. Diane had unfortunately heard about a notorious case in Chicago in which a sleeping child was taken from her bed, carried past her parents' room, and then murdered. Even when Diane was eight years old, Mom would often awaken in the middle of a cold winter night to see her shivering silently by the bedside, wanting to be near Mom for protection from the unseen terrors of the dark. As Diane reached puberty, she became increasingly round-shouldered, as if she were turning in upon herself for protection against the world.

The constant tension in our home, which only added to Diane's problems, was an inevitable result of Dad's eccentricities. It was almost impossible to avoid arguing with someone who had such strange ideas and habits. For a number of years, Dad drove his car on the wrong side of the highway to wear the tires evenly. He survived this practice only because there was so little traffic on the highways of southwest Nebraska. One day when I was riding with him, he was stopped by a highway patrolman, who assumed Dad was drunk because he had been driving all over the road. The patrolman was clearly perplexed when he could smell no alcohol on Dad's breath and finally let him go with a warning. Fortunately, Dad did not tell him his theory about wearing the tires evenly.

Dad made a fetish of accumulation. We would have been inundated by a sea of books, magazines, and newspapers had Mom not surreptitiously thrown out everything she thought he would not miss when his back was turned. During one period he subscribed to five daily newspapers, including the *New York Times*, and tried to keep them all. Dust-covered stacks of newspapers filled every corner of our basement. Whenever Dad left on business trips, Mom burned huge bonfires piled with as many papers and magazines as she could carry out of the basement, but it was a losing battle. It was particularly frustrating to her to try to keep the living room looking presentable when Dad was constantly bringing in stacks of books and papers. She always lamented that she felt as if she were doomed to clean the Augean stables for the rest of her life.

As the years passed, Dad's passion for book collecting intensified until he eventually owned nearly 11,000 volumes. The irony of it all was that Dad was a very slow reader and could not have read more than a book a fortnight. On the other hand, he had a certain familiarity with the general subjects of his books, and out of the surrounding stacks and clutter, he could always find for you any specific title. One of his friends remarked that no matter what topic you mentioned to my father, he would go home and return a little while later with a book upon the subject.

During the 1930s, Dad became a charter member of the Limited Edition Club, which printed a limited number of copies of various classics in beautiful editions. Those books were among his most prized possessions. As a child, I would study the titles in the glass-front book-cases, thinking that some day I would read all those stories that had to be wonderful because they were so specially bound. Since Dad always believed that if one was good, more was better, he decided in the late 1940s to subscribe to two more sets of these books to divide among us children.

Dad's obsession for acquiring books puzzled us all; I think it likely that he had repressed a strong interest in literature and history in order to please his father by becoming a businessman. Perhaps when he bought books, he persuaded himself that he would some day have time to read them. One of the only times I ever caught a glimpse of what went on inside my father's head was during a trip he made to New York with me when I was about to sail to France for a year's study at the Sorbonne. At the end of a leisurely meal in one of New York's penthouse restaurants, the conversation turned to my future plans and prospects. It seemed such a natural question that I asked Dad if he had ever wanted to pursue a different career. I'll never forget his brief and enigmatic answer: "I never felt I could tell my parents I wanted to do something else since my grades weren't as good as yours." Who could know what half-formulated, quickly aborted dreams lay hidden beneath his words?

CHAPTER THREE

Mom wanted desperately to have a new house, which was hardly unreasonable since Dad owned eight lumberyards. She always loved interior decoration and was in her element when she was selecting fabrics or choosing new furniture. Our farmhouse bungalow offered her little outlet for these interests, however, and was hardly the kind of home most families in our financial position would have owned. With only three bedrooms, it was too small for a family of six, so Mark slept in a corner of my parents' room for the first five years of his life until Kent left for college. At the age of ten, I decided that I no longer wanted to share a room with my sister, so I moved down to a corner of the basement.

The basement was unfinished and had only painted concrete walls and floors. My "bedroom" was in no way separated off from the rest of the basement. The closest thing I had to privacy was a call from the top of the stairs announcing that someone was about to come down. Since the foot of my bed was only a few feet from our coal furnace, coal dust made a constant cleaning problem. Every night I fell asleep smelling the acrid fumes from the bucket of clinkers cooling nearby. Mom tacked up some old sheets above the bed to hide the dusty, cobwebby rafters, but I was frequently horrified to see a huge spider scuttling across my bed.

Dad always told Mom to be patient, that another depression was right around the corner, so they could soon build a house for a fraction of the cost. Hence as a child I ended up with the confused impression that a depression was much to be desired. Mom waited a lifetime for the depression that never came, in whose imminence Dad never stopped believing.

There was a large hill south of town that Mom had chosen as just the place to build her dream house. We used to walk around the site, imagining where the house would be, where we could put a grape arbor, where a back terrace would overlook the winding canyons below. Finally, after several years of studying house plans, Mom realized with

a deep feeling of disappointment that Dad would never build her a new house.

Mom was not the only one who wanted a new home. Grandmother Krotter was tired of struggling to keep her large eleven-room house clean and felt very lonely living there. One afternoon when Dad and I were visiting her, she told him she wanted to build a small house where she could spend the remainder of her life. Dad gave her his all too familiar reasons why it was not economically justifiable for her to build her small house. As my grandmother sat there crying, my father withdrew into a stony silence behind his newspaper. She never got her new home, but she left more than $150,000 to her grandchildren when she died in 1951. A small fraction of that money would have built the house she wanted so much. Ironically enough, Grandmother Krotter herself helped nurture the philosophy that denied her the new home for which she longed. She used to tell me with pride how as a young woman she would wear the same two housedresses all year long so that her sons would some day have more money.

Although neither my grandmother nor my mother ever built the new houses they dreamed about, Dad did purchase for the family a beautiful log cabin in the town of Estes Park, high in the Rocky Mountains of Colorado. The large house built of tongue-and-groove logs had a huge field stone fireplace in the living room. From the front porch, there was an unsurpassed view of a dozen snow-capped peaks. The cabin itself was built in a large meadow bordered by tall Ponderosa pine trees and secluded in the middle of sixty acres on a mountainside.

Dad was always too busy to spend more than a few days a summer with us, but my mother, her parents, and we children enjoyed almost three months in Estes Park every summer. It was the escape valve that enabled Mom to accept her life with Dad in Palisade.

Estes Park seemed almost overpoweringly beautiful to me as a child, for I had nothing to compare it with but the prairies of Nebraska, where trees were so rare that you knew the shape of each one of them. The prairies were almost always dry and brown and austere; the fields crackled as you walked across them, filling the air with a dusty scent of dried weeds. There was a certain stark beauty to Nebraska, though, that I loved as I roamed the pastures and explored the meandering creek beyond our house. It was a beauty of understatement, while Estes Park, with its peaks and glaciers and rushing rivers, seemed all hyperbole. The meadows in Estes Park abounded in colorful wildflowers. In Nebraska the wildflowers were so scarce, I made a pilgrimage every April to a dry

canyon a mile beyond our farm to pick the blossoms from a few scrubby wild plum trees.

For all of us children, the cabin in Estes Park offered an escape from the stifling feeling we experienced growing up in a small town, where we had the impression we were living on the outermost fringe of the cultural and intellectual life we knew existed elsewhere. I can remember walking toward town one evening when I was a teenager and looking at that little village, with its Main Street so short that you could see right through town to the encircling hills beyond. In the enveloping darkness broken only by a handful of street lights and the scattered stars above the little grouping of stores and houses, I had the sense that the town was floating on the edge of some vast universe, cut off forever from the rest of the world. An intense feeling swept over me that I was trapped there and that the boundaries of those streets would be the limits of my achievements.

As we children grew up and left Palisade, we felt almost embarrassed to admit to our urban friends that we had grown up in a town of a few hundred people, but small-town life had certain advantages. For the study of human personality, nothing could compare with that small town where we knew everyone and all the details of their lives. We lived day in and day out with the whole gamut of human types—welfare recipients, farmers, their hired hands, shopkeepers, mechanics, and professionals.

Keenly aware of all that Palisade could not offer us, Mom did everything she could to enlarge our cultural opportunities. She had always been very interested in drama and had coached all of us in dramatic readings. To enable us to study with the best music teachers available, she drove us long distances to music lessons. My senior year in high school she drove me 300 miles round trip every two weeks so that I could study piano at Hastings College with a professor who had studied Bach with Albert Schweitzer. Mom even succeeded in finding me a violin teacher who had studied with one of the great European violinists in Prague before the First World War necessitated her return to her Nebraska home, where she married the owner of a service station in a small town located sixty miles from us. She was a woman of great style, and her living room decor, so unlike anything else in those little prairie towns, reflected the time she had studied in Europe.

Our school experience was not intellectually stimulating, but its very limitations had a positive aspect. I realized quite early that I had to

assume responsibility for my own education and started reading my way through the classics that were close at hand in Dad's library. The variety of experience offered by our small high school did give us some special opportunities. With only a dozen students in each class, almost everyone had to participate in all the various school activities, such as music, athletics, drama, and school publications. The junior and senior classes each gave a play every year, and if the class had eight boys and six girls, then the director searched for a script requiring that exact cast.

For most students, this total participation was a broadening experience, but not for Kent. He was an excellent actor and a good singer, but his total lack of athletic ability led to adjustment problems that plagued him for the rest of his life. One year he went out for football, although his slight build made him an unlikely candidate. After a week of practice, he decided he would rather quit than expose himself any longer to the ridicule of his brawnier teammates. Dad insisted, however, that he stay on the football team because he believed that once you started something you should not quit. Although he had experienced the same painful feelings of athletic failure as a boy, he could respond to Kent's problem only by making a virtue of sticking to something difficult in order to build character. Dad always pushed himself to the limit and expected the same of those around him. Relaxation and recreation were completely foreign to him; it was as if he had been tightly wound up as a child and set irrevocably in motion toward unquestioned goals.

By the time Kent was in high school, Mom had fallen into the habit of relying on him as a confidant because they both felt so frustrated trying to cope with Dad and small-town life. As the rest of us grew up, we fell into the same family pattern, forming a close-knit unit with Mom. We spent a great deal of time together because not only our money but also our intellectual and cultural interests isolated us from others in that small prairie town.

CHAPTER FOUR

In the summer of 1945, Mom suffered a miscarriage at Estes Park. Her parents and Aunt Thelma were spending the summer with us, and Dad happened to be spending a couple of days at the cabin when Mom suddenly started to hemorrhage. Our cabin was four miles from town, where there was a doctor, but no hospital. In the midst of the crisis, Dad simply drove off to Nebraska, leaving the others to get the doctor and cope with the situation. I was too young to realize what was happening and only heard a few sparse details of the crisis from Aunt Thelma many years later. What seemed to sum up the gravity of the situation was my grandfather's angry threat shouted after my father as he drove away from the cabin, "If I get my hands on him, I'll wring his neck."

Mom's next pregnancy was a successful one, and in 1947 my brother Mark was born, eight years my junior. Delighted that the new baby was a boy, Kent announced, "Now he can be the lumberman." Mark at once became the family pet, and none of us could help spoiling him. He was a special joy to my grandfather, to whom he formed a deep attachment, as I had done before him. Grandfather would have done anything for Mark. Every Saturday, while the rest of us spent the day taking music lessons in the nearby town of McCook, Grandfather made him a pumpkin pie because it was Mark's favorite food. Once again he became a substitute father, filling the same emotional void in Mark's life he had filled in mine.

The year that Mark started kindergarten, Kent entered Carleton College in Minnesota. Family trips to attend Parents' Day or other events were exciting escapes from the provincial atmosphere of Palisade to a world where ideas and academic pursuits were valued. On one memorable occasion, we all traveled to Carleton to hear Kent sing the role of the Lord High Chancellor in Gilbert and Sullivan's *Iolanthe*. He performed the famous rapid-fire nightmare song with great comic flare, as we all sat bursting with pride. It was a highlight in my brother's life that would contain few successes in the ensuing years. When he graduated, he had a degree in economics but no clear direction in life. He was sure of only one thing–he didn't want to enter Dad's business.

All career decisions were delayed when Kent was drafted into the army shortly after his graduation. Although he had dreaded the draft for years, he found his army experience to be much less traumatic than he had feared. Instead of being sent to fight in the Korean War, he spent his time as a clerk-typist at an army base in California.

After his discharge, Kent was still undecided about a career. Finally he decided to attend drama school in New York because he had always been very interested in the theater and had participated competently in leading roles in various amateur or college productions. Although Dad had always made clear his desire to have Kent enter the family business, he surprised us all by agreeing to send him to New York to study drama.

Unfortunately, Kent did not find himself in the theater. He was annoyed with his fellow actors and teachers because no one could give him a detailed intellectual description of how they expressed character or emotion. After a year in New York, he left the theater in his frustration with people who were simply acting without being able to explain "how" they acted.

Kent had become an increasingly abstract person. He constantly intellectualized life and detached himself from concrete experience, dwelling in a world of ideas from which he emerged less and less frequently. Much of his energy was spent trying to discover the Meaning of Life, a search probably related to his own unhappiness. Kent and Mom had an ongoing discussion about the search for the Meaning of Life. Kent insisted that you should have life all figured out before you embarked upon a career, marriage, and a family. Mom, on the other hand, kept telling him that you only learned about life by living it.

From adolescence on, Kent spent long hours investigating various schools of thought offering the answer to life. Mysticism always fascinated him. While still in high school, he ordered from a magazine ad a series of tiny blue paperback books by an author named E. Haldemann Julius, who wrote about the "secret path of life." When he was a freshman in college, Kent subscribed to a mail-order Yoga course. Failing to achieve the wonderful results promised in the prospectus, he wrote to the company to ask why things weren't working out according to plan. He carefully explained how he was getting up before 5 o'clock every morning to spend two hours doing the exercises, adding, ironically enough, given the time these exercises took away from his course work, that one of his objectives was to attain higher grades. The company wrote back urging him to be patient and continue through the rest of the lessons. A few weeks later Kent wrote them once again to complain that the system still wasn't working—his grades weren't improving.

One of the things that most typified Kent's approach to life was his attitude toward Mozart. With an air of intellectual superiority, he asserted that Mozart was "shallow," producing happy and frivolous music with no real meaning. He preferred instead the grandiose, soul-searching themes of Rachmaninoff.

Diane and I also attended Carleton College, where we were each elected to Phi Beta Kappa in our junior year. During the two years we overlapped at Carleton, we spent a lot of time together and even lived on the same dormitory floor during her senior year. Since my earliest memories, the relationship between Diane and me had been extremely close, and unlike most siblings, we never argued about anything. It was Diane who taught me to read when I was only three years old, and we enjoyed many happy times "playing house" in all the inviting spots of our sprawling farm, with its barn, hog house, chicken house, and clusters of large cottonwood trees that fueled our imagination. As we became older, we played music together. A fine pianist, Diane was always there to play my accompaniments or join me in playing violin and piano sonatas.

A change began to occur in our relationship, however, after I graduated from college in 1960. Having majored in mathematics, I spent a year studying at the Sorbonne on a National Science Foundation fellowship and also took advantage of the opportunity to study with Yvonne Astruc, one of the best violin teachers in Paris. After returning to the States, I got a master's degree in math but decided not to continue for a Ph.D. because I increasingly felt I had chosen the wrong field—my real interests lay in literature and history. When I was choosing my major in college, I had been too heavily influenced by my math professors, who praised my ability in the field. (I was a strong enough student to gain acceptance to the Ph.D. programs at both Harvard and Yale.) My professors and others took the view that it was so important to encourage gifted women to enter fields like math and physics that they didn't pause to realize that strong talent in a field is not the only reason to pursue it.

After I got my master's degree in math, I took a job teaching math at Emmanuel College in Boston. I also took violin lessons at the New England Conservatory, which had been one of the attractions of working in Boston. The second year I was there I took a literature course at Boston University in a further effort to decide if I should change fields, and I also focused more of my time on violin study. While I was in Boston, a cellist friend from Carleton College suggested I come over to play trios with two of her fellow grad students at MIT, who both played the piano. That's how I met Wells Johnson. I often suspected that many men thought I was too tall or too smart, but that was not a problem for Wells. He was 6'2" and had been a starter on his high school basketball team. Like me, he loved nature and loved to hike, so we shared many common interests. In many ways, Wells reminded me of my grandfather. He was much more interested in people and ordinary life than my father and brothers were. My brother Kent and sister Diane enjoyed long philosophical discussions, but Wells saw little point in trying to decide how many angels could dance on the head of a pin. He was firmly planted in the real world.

Wells and I were married in Estes Park in 1964 and held the reception at our cabin. At the end of the summer, we drove to Brunswick, Maine, where Wells was starting a job as a math professor at Bowdoin College. We were eager to start a family, so I decided to switch careers and become a private violin teacher. Giving lessons in my own home with a babysitter to watch the children worked out very well. I also played in the Portland Symphony for several years.

Diane started teaching piano in Colorado at that point, and we continued to see each other during summer vacations at the cabin in Estes Park. Our relationship changed with my marriage, however. Diane didn't feel all that comfortable around most men, and I think she felt that Wells came between us. After Wells and I left for our honeymoon, Kent, Mark, and Diane all went out to dinner together in order to, as one of them later told me, "console ourselves for having lost our sister."

* * * * *

After we three older children left home, Mom felt more sharply than ever the limitations of Palisade. She had never really been comfortable there and had always sought out any cultural or intellectual opportunities she could find. When one of the many new ministers who filled our pulpit for a short period of years saw her for the first time, he said, "Thank heavens I met you; I thought I was going to have to talk about the pigs and the crops for the rest of my life!"

The pettiness of small town life particularly disturbed and depressed Mom. Most conversation turned quickly to gossip, and every aspect of the personality and actions of everyone in town was minutely scrutinized and, more often than not, was roundly criticized. If anyone attempted to have an extramarital affair, their efforts at concealment were futile because no man could park his car at a woman's house without neighbors on all sides noting his time of arrival and departure. It wasn't simply major infractions of the town's standards that invoked critical comment. On the way home from social evenings, women would criticize the hostess if they had noticed a trace of dust in the corner of a room. At one club meeting, the woman sitting beside Mom turned back the hem of a nearby curtain and whispered, "I wouldn't hem my curtains that way, would you?"

Mom found some outlet for her interests in the nearby town of McCook, where she was active in the American Association of University Women and was an officer for the Community Concert Association. She loved music and for many years sang solos and directed the Methodist choir in Palisade. The height of the social and cultural life of Palisade was the Eastern Star, the branch of the Masonic Lodge that includes women. For want of anything else to do, Mom was active in it. I can remember her saying that if she didn't belong to the Eastern Star, she would never have a chance to dress up and go out in the evening. Although Dad would occasionally take her to McCook to attend a dinner-lecture club, her enjoyment of those evenings was always spoiled by her extreme embarrassment when Dad raised his hand during the question-and-answer period. No lecturer on any subject ever escaped Dad's eternal question, "What is your opinion of the gold standard?"

At that time in our lives, Dad's obsession with gold seemed just an embarrassing foible. By the time its destructive influence became apparent, it was too late to reverse the damage already done to those he loved.

CHAPTER FIVE

By the time Mark was ready to begin high school, Palisade's decline was apparent even to my loyal father, who wanted him to have the best education possible. Having read that New Trier High School on the Chicago North Shore was the best public high school in the country, he decided Mark should go there. Our family never did anything in the usual fashion; Dad thought Mom should set up housekeeping in Illinois for four years while Mark attended New Trier. She wanted to rent an apartment, but Dad was convinced that Mark's right to attend the school would be greater if they owned property, so he bought a house for them. The irony escaped none of us that Dad had previously refused to give Mom and Grandmother Krotter the new houses they longed for and now almost casually decided to buy a house that Mom didn't want.

Mom was probably secretly delighted with the opportunity to escape at last from Palisade. The Chicago North Shore offered many opportunities for a woman of her tastes and ability. Before long she was singing in a fine church choir, participating in two literature groups, and taking a French course.

These were four long and lonely years for Dad, however, who was left all alone in Palisade, albeit by his own design. The whole strange plan showed his great capacity for self-sacrifice, his belief in the importance of a fine education, and his ambition for his children. At the same time, it reflected the fact that he would rather see Mark obtain the finest education possible than have the pleasure of living with him through those years.

The problem for Mom, of course, arose when Mark graduated from high school. He was leaving for Yale and she was leaving for Palisade, and the contrast could not have been sharper. She might have saved her sanity had she cut loose at that point and told Dad she wasn't coming home. Whether she went back because she was too kind and decent a person to hurt Dad or because she was too passive to assert her own desires, I will never know. She had always been keenly aware of how frustrating it was for Dad to try to hold together the declining business empire he had inherited from his father whom he had idolized. Perhaps she did not want to add one more bitter disappointment to his life by leaving him. Once again, money may have been involved in her decision. Dad had transferred many of his business interests into her name so that on paper she was a wealthy woman, but she never felt she had a right to the money unless she took Dad with it.

The day Mark left for Yale an incident occurred that reminded Mom all too clearly what it would be like to live with Dad again. We were all out at Estes Park before Mark's departure; even Dad had come in late the night before Mark was to leave. When the rest of us returned from taking Mark to the bus, we found Dad sitting in the kitchen, surrounded by pails and boxes of wild plums he had just unloaded from the trunk of his car. He was beaming with pride as he showed Mom all these wild plums he had picked along a Nebraska roadside. Of course, he expected her to drop everything else and make great quantities of jam and jelly. His project couldn't have caught Mom at a worse time because she felt bereft to have her last child leaving home and wanted to relax during her final week at the cabin before she returned to face life in Palisade.

For days the kitchen was converted into a jam factory, with plums boiling away on the stove. Dad had brought along an old colander with a wooden mallet to force fruit puree through the holes. In our bedroom adjacent to the kitchen, Wells and I were kept up late at night and awakened early in the morning by an incessant thumping sound as Dad worked the wooden mallet up and down in the colander. After a few days, we had a lifetime supply of wild plum jam. Unfortunately, no one but Dad liked this bland jam.

After Mark left for Yale, he began to distance himself from the family. Every summer he went to summer school instead of coming to Estes Park, even though he had always loved to hike and fish there. After his freshman year, he never went home for Christmas. His second year at Yale, I went down to spend an afternoon with him during the Christmas vacation. I couldn't imagine why he would want to stay in his lonely room in a deserted college at Christmas, so I finally asked him why he didn't go home. He replied that it bothered him too much to see Mom and Dad arguing.

Mark's statement reminded me of a particularly upsetting dispute that had occurred a few years earlier when he was attending high school in Illinois. We had as usual all returned to Nebraska for Christmas, and on Christmas Day Dad had decided we should all drive down to McCook for the evening to visit a doctor there who had made a casual inquiry about Mark's school. Dad was sure this doctor wanted to learn all about the school so he too could send his wife and son to the Chicago North Shore. Mom, however, knew this was a most unlikely possibility and said that we couldn't all six descend upon someone unannounced on Christmas night. Dad was furious and shouted at Mom as he stormed out of the house. This argument, like so many others, seemed to arise inevitably because Dad just couldn't see a situation the way anyone else would. His odd perspective on everything in life made these constant clashes with his family almost unavoidable.

When Mom did go back to Palisade in 1965, it was not to the house where I had grown up. While I was away at college, our family had moved from our country house to Dad's old family home in town, vacant since my grandmother's death. Dad found it difficult to part with anything, including houses. He left the country or "south" house fully furnished, and for almost two decades he kept the furnace running in an unoccupied house.

Soon after returning home, Mom launched a complete redecorating project for the town house, managing for at least a few months to fill the sudden emptiness in her life caused not only by the departure of her last child but also by her removal from the sophisticated Chicago North Shore to rural Nebraska. Palisade was now an even less interesting place than it had been when she arrived in 1930. With the decline of business opportunities, most of the better-educated and enterprising people had moved away. There were exceptions, of course, but most of the people Mom had found congenial were now gone. She often remarked that some day there would be no one left in Palisade but the Krotters and the coyotes. When the drugstore finally closed, it was a depressing event. No longer did Mom have even the small pleasure of walking over to town to buy a cold drink and talk to the woman who worked at the soda fountain.

Dad's stubborn attitudes continued to make life difficult for Mom. We had always suffered with coal furnaces because he sold coal; finally we were almost the only people in town without an oil burner. Coal dust and smoke permeated even the upstairs rooms, coating furniture, floor, and walls with a thin grey layer that made housekeeping a constant struggle. At last Mom thought she had talked Dad into installing an oil burner to replace their old coal furnace. She went to California for a month to visit Aunt Thelma with the understanding that Dad would have the oil burner installed in her absence. To her dismay, she returned to find a new coal furnace in place. Dad was always very eccentric about how he spent money, buying things he wanted in large quantities. Mom once made a remark about the high cost of a can of pecans, and thereafter Dad bought pecans in twenty-five pound bags. Of course, they became rancid before we even used half a bag, and Mom had to throw the rest of them out.

During this period, Dad became fearful that Cross and Blackwell was going to discontinue his favorite kind of orange marmalade, so he ordered thirty cases. Now Mom had to find a place to store these thirty boxes of jam. Out of curiosity she decided to check out Dad's rate of orange marmalade consumption and discovered that a jar lasted him about a month. Since a case contained twelve jars, he had a thirty-year supply, but it seemed unlikely either he or the orange marmalade would last that long.

In so many ways, it seemed Mom was fighting an impossible battle against the growing accumulation. When she had cleaned out the town house a few years earlier, she had found dozens of old canning jars in the basement fruit room. She arranged for some people named Wilson to take a lot of trash away, including the jars. As it turned out, the Wilsons took the jars home and stored them in their storm cellar. When they died years later, Dad bought their house because he dealt widely in real estate. As he looked around the property, his attention fell on the dusty old canning jars in their storm cellar. Viewing them as a find, he took them home to Mom, saying they might be useful some day.

But by far the most disquieting factor in Mom's life after she returned to Palisade was Dad's growing mania for amassing gold and silver coins. Dad was extremely conservative politically and studied national fiscal policy closely. He was convinced that only a return to the gold standard would save the country from the ravages of inflation and economic disaster. In the late 1950s, he realized that it was very likely that the value of the silver in war nickels and other silver coins would soon exceed their face value. Accordingly, he started gathering together coins as fast as he could. Storage became a problem almost at once. Now it was more difficult than ever to clean under the beds because they concealed not only cartons of books but also heavy boxes of coins. Dresser drawers, the top shelves of cupboards, every available corner was pressed into service as boxes of nickels arrived at the post office from vending machine operators, and heavy canvas bags of quarters came via railroad express.

As the size of his hoard grew ever larger, Dad became concerned about better storage, but he wouldn't have dreamed of putting his gold and silver in a bank vault. Over and over again he told us that in an economic crisis, the government would have a policeman with a gun barring the entrance to every bank vault.

For a few years, Dad used the south house to store most of the coins, but he was increasingly concerned that neighborhood children or burglars might break into the uninhabited house. He eventually decided to consolidate at least some of the silver coins he had accumulated and bury them. But every gold bug has a problem. How do you bury your gold or silver without being seen or heard? If you go out in your backyard in the middle of the night and start digging, a restless neighbor may hear you. Dad had a remarkably convenient solution to this problem because the long brick garage near the town house contained a large back room with a dirt floor. This room was located across the alley from the back of the lumberyard, and a table saw was kept there, which men from the yard occasionally came over to use. In addition, all sorts of metal objects like old wheels and pipe were stored there. This was an ideal place for Dad to bury his hoard because he could dig without being seen. Even then he didn't want to dig during the day, when a passerby might hear him or someone might come over to use the saw, so he decided to carry out the whole operation at night. He had not told Mom of his plans, however, so she became very worried when he failed to come home by midnight one night.

Around 4 A.M., Dad came in the house so totally exhausted that Mom was alarmed. He explained that he had been digging a large hole in the garage and then going back and forth to the south house to bring the silver coins to town to bury them. The only reason he had come into the house was to get a drink and collect the coins he had concealed in the attic and various other hiding places. With dawn only two hours away, he had been working frantically to finish. In order to hide the signs of his digging, he had dragged an enormous work table away from the spot where he wanted to bury the coins. When he was all done, he would have to drag it back into position. The whole operation of moving the table, digging the hole, and carrying dozens of heavy boxes of coins was very risky for Dad because he had suffered a heart attack a few years earlier. If he had collapsed in the hole on top of his silver, he might not have been found for days. He did, however, complete his operation before sunrise, and the cache remained undisturbed for the next ten years.

Although Dad did not talk openly about his coin hoarding, several people knew about it because all those boxes and bags of coins arriving by mail and railroad excited curiosity. Dad also had various friends and acquaintances saving coins for him, so word spread in this fashion. As the size of the hoard increased, Mom began to be frightened about the possibility of robbery. Dad frequently went away on business trips, leaving her alone in that large house to worry that someone would break in and force her to divulge where all the coins were hidden.

Dad's business trips frequently took him to Omaha, where he would often drop in to chat with Warren Buffett because he had been a good friend of Warren's father, Howard, a U.S. congressman. I can remember many occasions when Dad told us that Warren was trying to talk him into investing in his new company but he had told Warren that he was putting all his money into amassing silver coins. Our lives would have played out far differently had Dad only taken Warren Buffett's advice instead of putting all his money in a hole in the ground.

And all the while that Dad was collecting some 200,000 silver nickels, he would still make Mom walk five blocks just to save putting a nickel in a parking meter when they visited Lincoln or Denver.

CHAPTER SIX

The cloud of the Vietnam War hung over Mark's graduation from Yale in 1968. Because he was strongly opposed to the conflict, he decided to move to Canada. Before the draft had reached him, he crossed the border, renounced his American citizenship, and immediately applied for landed-immigrant status. Having left the United States without breaking any draft laws, he was free to return after he received his Canadian citizenship in five years, even had amnesty never been declared.

There had been endless discussions within the family about Mark's intentions, and he left with the support of his parents and siblings. Originally, Dad was unaware of his plans, and the rest of us worried about what his reaction might be because he was extremely conservative and was an odd cross between a hawk and an isolationist. When Mark finally broke the news to him, however, he was very supportive and gave him money to attend law school in Canada.

When word got around Palisade that Mark Krotter had gone to Canada, the town was scandalized. Anonymous letters appeared in the area newspapers, and my parents couldn't leave the house without encountering sarcastic remarks. The local lawyer, who was Dad's best friend, asserted, "Mark is no better than a Communist." Mom had to fight back tears when Dad's cousin launched into a tirade and called Mark a coward. Mark had only to imagine what people in Palisade might think about his actions. Mom and Dad had to live with the revulsion of public opinion in a tiny town in the area of the country where support was strongest for U.S. policy in Vietnam. And after the initial outraged expressions of disapproval, Mark became a nonperson for Palisade, and no one ever asked my parents about him.

Unfortunately, the emotional strain Mark's departure caused my Mom was soon compounded by a far greater blow. When she visited Kent in the fall of 1969 in New Jersey, where he was working as a computer programmer, she found his apartment a total mess and soon realized he had developed an alcohol problem. When Kent returned to Nebraska to spend Christmas, however, Mom and Diane managed to keep Dad from realizing he was drinking. Mom always had a tendency simply to worry about problems, instead of facing them head on and deciding on the best course of action. She let knowledge of Kent's situation just fester in her mind, not even sharing the information with me.

In late March of 1970, I received a phone call from Dad saying Mom had had a nervous breakdown. He explained that he had left her in a mental hospital in Omaha and then returned to Palisade, six hours away. The next morning I flew to Omaha with my six-month-old baby, leaving Wells to take care of our three year old. I arrived that evening, hurriedly dropped the baby off at a friend's home, and went directly to the hospital. It was a gloomy old place with dark corridors of grey brick that made me feel even more discouraged. Like most mothers, mine had been to me such a symbol of strength, authority, and love that it was extremely unnerving to see her reduced to a quivering state of extreme anxiety. Back and forth she paced from one side of the bleak room to the other, wringing her hands and chanting over and over, "What are we going to do, what are we going to do?" Of course, the same question was racing through my mind, but I attempted to reassure her that we could find help.

Mom's anxiety at that moment focused on financial matters; she kept worrying that we didn't have enough money, that the hospital would be too expensive. Her financial worries seemed especially ironic when I thought of all the gold and silver Dad had hidden away at home. No matter what I said, however, she remained distraught, and I left the hospital feeling as if a part of the solid world had fallen away. One usually awakens from a bad dream and experiences a sense of relief that none of it was true. That night I kept awakening to find that the present reality was worse than any nightmare.

Diane flew in the following morning to join me, and we arranged an appointment with Mom's psychiatrist. Our first negative impression was only confirmed when we learned to our dismay that with only a day's acquaintance with the case, he was urging Dad to sign a release for electric shock treatments. We objected emphatically to this course, but when we returned to the hotel and called Dad, we learned he had already signed and mailed off the release. A further check with the hospital gave us the frightening information that they intended to begin shock treatments early the next morning. Diane and I were both aghast at this prospect, having assumed that shock treatments were a remnant from a less enlightened period. The thought that some irreversible damage would be done to the mother we loved so much without our having the power to prevent it terrified us and left us feeling powerless. In desperation we decided to move Mom to Denver, where Diane could supervise her treatment. Through a friend we made contact with an excellent Denver psychiatrist named James Galvin, and we decided to fly out immediately to put Mom under his care. Fortunately, we were able to persuade Dad to let us do this.

When I called the Omaha psychiatrist to tell him our decision and to request medication to calm Mom for the flight, he told me in icy tones that we were foolish not to give her immediate shock treatments, and he insisted we were taking a great risk removing her from the hospital. He refused to give her any medication and said he washed his hands of the whole affair. Of course, his words made us all the more fearful about the step we were taking, but they did not deter us.

With very mixed emotions, we walked out of the hospital door with Mom late that same afternoon. We experienced an enormous sense of escape, as though we had just saved her from a terrible fate. Yet at the same time we felt very apprehensive to be heading out into the unknown region of mental illness with a patient whose behavior we had no way of predicting, with our attention also required by a small baby. As we walked out the door of the hospital, Mom said, "I hope you girls know what you're doing." We weren't sure we did.

Later that evening we all arrived in Denver and went to Diane's apartment. That night was very scary. I kept having nightmares that Mom was committing suicide, even though I had cleaned out the pills and razor blades from the medicine cabinet. My fears were unfounded, however, for underneath all her crazy talk and behavior, Mom still loved us very much. She never availed herself of that easy exit despite her suffering over the ensuing years because she was afraid it would hurt her family. She once said to Diane, "You know, you can't even die without someone tripping over your body."

When morning finally arrived, I walked to the grocery to buy some food. When I returned, Mom was in a state of panic at the extravagance of my routine purchases. As I unpacked the bags, she would pick up a can of tuna or a box of rice, exclaiming, "We can't afford this, Alison, where are we going to get the money to pay for all this?" Even the bunch of daffodils I had bought to cheer us up only added to her anxiety. It was hard for me to try to relax and nurse my baby as she paced constantly up and down the living room, wringing her hands and saying, "What are we going to do, what are we going to do?" At one end of her path was a huge vase on a pedestal, and she stopped once and put her hands on it, swaying it back and forth. I held my breath, fearing she was about to break it, but she suddenly turned and resumed her fretful circuit.

That afternoon we all went to see Dr. Galvin for the first time. It was difficult to try in the space of a half hour to explain to him the frustrations that had filled Mom's life, but he was extremely intelligent, kind, and sympathetic, and he seemed to grasp the picture quickly. Although Mom always had an extreme distaste for telling her problems to anyone outside the family, she did like Dr. Galvin.

Dr. Galvin immediately started Mom on a medication that had a slight calming effect. We had expected him to rehospitalize her, but he thought it would be best for her to stay with Diane in her apartment. That turned out to be a great mistake. Only Diane and I knew what hell it was to share a one-bedroom apartment with Mom. It's not easy to sleep at night with someone half-crazy in the next bed. Even though you are rationally convinced that they are by nature nonviolent, as you lie in the dark your imagination takes over and you start at every sound.

Waking hours spent with Mom were not much better. At mealtime she would offer little conversation, wringing her hands constantly and fretting over the cost of the food so that we could not even enjoy what we were eating. When we tried to relax in the living room by reading a book or watching television, Mom's incessant pacing made it impossible for us to forget our problems for even a moment.

At the end of a week, I returned to Maine to take care of my family and resume teaching my violin students. I left with an intense feeling of relief and escape, combined with a sense of guilt that I had to leave Diane to cope with Mom single-handedly. She took care of Mom in that apartment for two months, leaving during the day to teach at her piano studio. No one could have shown more devotion than she did that spring, but it was a grueling experience.

From a psychological viewpoint, an odd reversal of roles had occurred. As an emotionally troubled child, Diane had required much more of Mom's attention than the rest of us. When she was a teenager, Diane suffered greatly from homesickness. Any camp stay was a trying experience because she felt miserable for most of the time. When Diane went off to college, she was so incapacitated by homesickness that Mom had to spend a couple of weeks at Carleton to encourage her to stay in school. There would be many more times over the years when Mom would go to Diane's rescue. When she was lonely in a new situation, Mom would visit her. Whenever Diane moved into a new apartment, she helped her fix it up. Never a practical person, Diane depended on family members to nail up her pictures, organize her kitchen, and hang her curtains. She drove for a few months at age sixteen and then let others chauffeur her around for the next twenty years, only learning to drive again in her late thirties.

Now the situation was peculiarly reversed; instead of Mom taking care of Diane, Diane was doing everything for Mom. It was two months of extreme and unremitting psychological strain for Diane, and in the end her gallant sacrifice achieved nothing. Mom became much worse after several weeks and developed a feeling of paranoia that forced Dr. Galvin to hospitalize her after all. He had told us originally that shock treatments were "on the way out," but he now decided there was no alternative but to try them. We did some research and discovered to our great surprise that shock treatments were still widely used in cases of serious mental illness, so we finally acquiesced. The treatments did produce a temporary improvement in Mom's condition, but she continued to alternate between normal and abnormal periods for the next fourteen years.

During this hospitalization, Dad came to visit Mom, bringing her distressing news of his latest project. Our town house in Palisade was surrounded by a large and beautiful lawn that Grandmother Krotter had carefully nurtured for half a century. Over the last few years, however, Dad had become impatient with the task of hiring someone to mow the lawn. Now he horrified Mom by announcing that he had scalped off the top four inches of Kentucky bluegrass and replaced it by buffalo grass, the wiry, matted, grey-green grass the pioneers had found covering the treeless prairies when they arrived in Nebraska. No one but Dad would have dreamed of using this scrubby turf for a residential lawn. He was pleased, however, that it did not have to be watered and also did not have to be mowed because it never grew more than an inch high. Even the buffalo grass didn't thrive on neglect, however. To the chagrin of the neighbors, the yard was filled for many years with weeds competing with a few clumps of straggly buffalo grass. To make matters worse, our house was right next to Main Street, so everyone walked or drove by the yard on their way to the post office to collect their morning mail. In a town that loved to gossip, our family provided more than its share of incidents to enliven conversation over a cup of coffee or a game of pool. Of course, Mom was extremely upset to hear that Dad had wrecked the lawn, but I suspect he was too obtuse to notice how disturbed she was. Perhaps the buffalo grass project was itself a result of his inability to cope with Mom's illness and her departure from Palisade.

When Mom was released from the hospital in late June, we took her to Estes Park for the summer. Dad had promised to come out in early July for their wedding anniversary to take Mom and Aunt Thelma to Central City to see a pair of operas; they planned to spend a night in a hotel between performances. We all awaited his arrival one evening and finally got a call about 11 P.M. that he had been delayed and would arrive sometime in the middle of the night.

We were not surprised to hear Dad would be so late. Whenever he made a trip, he stopped along the way to try to collect money on old bills owed to his lumberyards. He could find someone who owed him money in almost any corner of Nebraska or Colorado. Sometimes they would pay up just to avoid having Dad pursue them for the next ten years. On one occasion when he stopped at a farmhouse to collect a bill, the woman told him her husband was not there. Dad decided just to wait a few hours to see if the man appeared. After a couple of hours, another man, clearly not the woman's husband, emerged from the house and told Dad to get the hell out of there.

On this occasion on the eve of the opera trip, Dad appeared at about 2 A.M., disturbing Mom's sleep. The next morning we were all awakened at 7 A.M. by a call from Dad's business partner in Palisade, who informed him that a house he owned had just been sold and that the new owners wanted to take possession the next day. Dad immediately began to worry because a boy who had lived in the house had a friend who had stolen some things from our south house. Believing that some of these unrecovered objects might have ended up in the house being sold, Dad decided to return immediately to Palisade on the fool's errand of searching through the house. Our protestations about how disappointed Mom and Aunt Thelma would be if the opera trip were suddenly canceled were in vain. At breakfast Dad announced to Mom that he was leaving for Palisade within an hour.

CHAPTER SEVEN

Mom was not our only problem. Kent was unemployed, so that summer Diane and I decided to see if we could help him. At that point, I only knew that Kent had lost his job and was having some psychological problems. Diane knew that he had a drinking problem but did not inform me, thinking it was his business to tell me if he wanted me to know. Many of my decisions concerning him would have been different had I known that he was an alcoholic. At the very least, I would have hesitated to bring him to Denver, as we soon did, because his erratic behavior there would affect both Mom and Diane. I might also have opted for a different form of treatment. As it was, Diane and I thought Dr. Galvin was just the kind of person to whom Kent would relate well. We discussed the matter with Dr. Galvin, who was confident he could help Kent and thereby help Mom. When we called Kent, he readily agreed to the idea.

We had a certain logistics problem getting Kent from New Jersey to Colorado because he needed money to cover moving expenses and some bills. Going to Dad for the money would have meant explaining to him that Kent was having some serious problems. We weren't yet ready to do that. For want of a better solution, I offered to lend Kent the money to move west. We had a long argument over the phone about how much money he would require. He did own a considerable number of Franklin Mint silver coins that he had purchased in a distorted desire either to emulate Dad or to outdo him. As with all Kent's abortive attempts to imitate Dad, this one was doomed to failure because Franklin Mint coins were hardly the best way to invest in silver. I suggested he sell his coins and then draw on me for the remainder of his needs, but I also expressed my concern about loaning him a large portion of our savings because we had children to raise. He offered an odd non sequitur, saying, "I would have liked to get married and have children too!" Then he suggested that it was Dad's fault that he wasn't married, asserting that if Dad had supplied him with more money, he would have been able to get married. "But Kent," I replied, "almost everyone else in the world thinks they can afford to marry without getting money from their parents." His answer was, "I'm not anyone else; I'm Kent Krotter."

Kent's financial relationship to Dad was a complicated one because Grandmother Krotter had left sizable amounts of money in trust for each of her grandchildren, payable at age thirty-five. This was a tax-saving arrangement Dad had engineered, and he as trustee simply continued to keep the money invested in his businesses. That would obviously have been my grandmother's intention; the last thing she would have wanted was for Dad to be forced to liquidate businesses to pay off the trusts.

During the period before his alcoholic decline, Kent and I had long discussions about this trust fund. When he insisted to me that he wanted immediate payment, even though his computer programming job paid him a good salary, I asked, "Do you really want Dad to have to sell a lumberyard at much too low a price just to be able to pay you right away?" His reply was, "Well, I would like him to at least face the facts and admit he can't pay me my money." That kind of talk made me suspect that Kent wanted to hurt or embarrass Dad.

Kent always seemed to have a tremendous need to prove himself his father's business equal, and this desire would take two forms. On the one hand, he would spend large amounts of time and money trying to beat Dad at his own game. For a number of years, he invested in the stock market on a purely technical basis, plotting graphs every night to decide when he should buy and sell. Once I asked him what was manufactured by one of the companies whose stock he owned. He replied that he didn't know and said that this fact was not relevant in a technical approach to the market. Dad was just the opposite, investing from a strictly fundamentalist approach, studying the annual reports of corporations and checking their lists of assets and liabilities carefully. He would have been horrified with the idea of purchasing stock in a company when one knew nothing but the graph of its prices. It is safe to assume Kent did not make any money this way because he would have been eager to tell us had he done so.

Kent seemed too inclined to focus on those business areas in which Dad was not making money, so that he could feel that Dad was not the great business genius, forever superior to his son. Kent almost relished the fact that our lumberyards were not making a profit instead of feeling sorry for Dad having to cope with a declining business environment. It always struck me as unfortunate that a thirty-five-year-old man was still living his life in reaction to his father. We were all painfully aware of Dad's shortcomings as a parent, but there was no reason for Kent to give up on life just because he didn't have an ideal father.

The outcome of all this financial and psychological entanglement was that Kent would not sell his silver coins, so I had to lend him $1,500 so that he could move west. Because our relationship had been close when we were growing up, I wanted to do what I could to help.

All through July we waited for Kent to move out of his apartment, not yet realizing the tremendous inertia an alcoholic can develop. We kept calling to ask when he was coming, and he kept saying that he didn't have his things organized and packed yet. Finally, we suggested that he simply turn the key on the apartment and walk out, leaving his stuff behind. At last in early August, he managed to load his belongings into a U-Haul trailer and headed for Colorado, sleeping in his car along the way.

Early one morning we were awakened by a knock on the door of the cabin. There stood a sheepish Kent, who said, "I was trying to drive a U-Haul trailer up the hill, but the back wheel slipped off the road. I've got to call a wrecker." A wrecker finally succeeded in getting the trailer onto the road, and Kent headed off to Denver, where Diane had rented an apartment for him. During the course of the morning, I thought once that I smelled alcohol on his breath, but I found it hard to imagine he would be drinking. When I mentioned my concerns to Wells, he said I had probably smelled shaving lotion on Kent. To add to all the tension that day, Mom kept pacing the floor of the cabin, saying, "What are we going to do, what are we going to do?" There were times like this when Mom's words seemed all too appropriate, even if they resulted from her mental illness.

After settling into his apartment, Kent began to see Dr. Galvin, with whom he initially felt a great rapport. Soon after his arrival, Diane, Mom, and I made a trip to Denver to consult with Dr. Galvin about Mom's living arrangements for the fall. As Kent was driving us to a restaurant one evening, he mistakenly assumed he was on a one-way street and started down the wrong lane of a two-way street. It was a dangerous mistake in heavy city traffic, and during the course of the evening I began to wonder if he might be drinking. When I confronted Diane with my suspicions later that night, she admitted she had known since Christmas that he had an alcohol problem. I was dismayed that she hadn't shared that crucial information with me; it would certainly have affected my willingness to lend Kent money to make the trip west.

When Kent found out that I knew he had a drinking problem, he said to me, "I wouldn't want you to get the impression I'm an alcoholic, Alison; I just drink to calm my nerves." Later on, as I read more about alcoholism, I learned how typical his denial was.

Although we knew Kent owed some money, he had concealed from us the fact that he was thousands of dollars in debt. No longer able to bear even looking at the bills, he just piled up unopened mail. Once we learned his debts totaled more than $4,000, we had to inform Dad of the whole situation. He was understandably very upset but agreed to pay Kent's debts out of his trust fund. A few weeks later, however, he told Diane and me that he was going to cut Kent out of his will. We suggested he not take any precipitous action, but the following summer he disinherited Kent.

As usual, Dad was not sensitive to the human problems involved. He suggested that because Kent was unemployed, he would pay him to clean out the septic tank at our cabin. This job consisted of digging a long trench in the rocky hillside and then lifting out buckets of raw sewage from the tank to bury in the trench. Since the project required a strong stomach and considerable exertion, it was hardly the thing to suggest to someone in a state of deep depression. Of course, all of us but Dad thought the idea was ludicrous. Fortunately, we prevailed against him and hired a tank truck to pump out the septic tank.

A week or so after Kent moved to Colorado, Dad and he both came to Estes Park for the weekend, and I attempted to mediate between them. On a long walk down our winding road bordered with tall pine trees, Kent and I argued all the issues at stake. Kent took the position that his problems would be solved if Dad would just pay over all his inheritance from Grandmother Krotter. "If Dad doesn't give me that money, I'll have to keep going through hell. It's to the point where I almost hate him," he complained bitterly. His present situation was not Dad's responsibility, I argued, unless one wanted to assert àn unrelenting psychological determinism. I also tried to convince him that it was essential for his self-respect and well-being, as well as his economic future, for him to get back to work. Dad had agreed to pay Kent's living expenses and psychiatrist bills out of his trust fund, and we all believed it was important not to dissipate the rest of the trust money by turning it over to Kent in his present state. It was disturbing to see, however, the extent to which Kent refused to accept responsibility for his own life, shifting all his faults onto Dad's shoulders, an attitude that decreased significantly his chances to recover.

CHAPTER EIGHT

It was impossible for Mom to go back to Palisade. Dr. Galvin, Diane, and I all agreed on that. She felt guilty about leaving Dad, but she knew she was simply beyond coping with him. Both Mom and Kent found it difficult, though, to free themselves psychologically from Dad. It was not easy for them to reject a man whose intentions were basically good, even though his ideas and actions were insensitive and irritating in a way that caused enormous frustration to those who tried to love him. Diane had her own theory that Mom felt she could escape from Dad only by being crazy.

It seemed best for Mom to rent an apartment in Denver, where she could see Diane regularly and continue treatment with Dr. Galvin. We looked at all sorts of apartments, but Mom was in such a low mood she didn't really like anything. The decision was not an easy one, but at last we found a good apartment in a downtown high-rise, with easy access to stores and restaurants. Of course, an apartment in a high-rise seemed less than ideal for a person who might be feeling suicidal, but other apartments we had considered contained gas stoves, which could offer an even easier exit. Mom liked the high-rise apartment the best of all the ones we had seen, so we went back to Diane's apartment to consider whether to sign a lease the next day. Diane and I finally decided to have Mom take the apartment, even though she was feeling very anxious about the whole situation.

That night I was sharing the bedroom at Diane's apartment with Mom. Suddenly I awakened to see her in the middle of the darkened room, jumping up and down and flailing her arms wildly about. It was an unnerving sight, but fortunately I was able to persuade her to get back into bed. Although she couldn't tell me what was wrong, her distress seemed clearly linked to the imminent decision to rent the apartment.

The next morning Diane and I decided to consult further with Dr. Galvin before signing a year's lease on an expensive apartment. We both had serious doubts about whether Mom could function independently in her own apartment. Dr. Galvin, however, said that during Mom's last visit with him, she herself had decided it would be best to get an apartment. He thought that regardless of her irrational behavior in the middle of the night, the fact that she had "made a decision" meant that she would be able to cope, so we relied upon his professional judgment. That afternoon we had Mom sign the lease. Unfortunately, it soon became apparent that we should have followed our own instincts instead of listening to Dr. Galvin.

We started off that fall with Mom set up in her apartment and Kent in his. There were a couple of basement rooms in Diane's apartment, so she agreed to let Kent move a couch and lots of his books into her basement because his own place was so small. As it turned out, he just holed up down there and drank. When Diane came back exhausted from a long day of piano teaching, she never knew if she would find Kent drunk, dead, or alive in her basement. Once she found him passed out in her upstairs study with a cigarette hole burned in the floor beside him. Dr. Galvin's initial evaluation was that Kent was a very intelligent person with a great deal of potential, and he was confident he could help him. As the months went by and Kent remained unemployed and continued to drink, Dr. Galvin began to take a dimmer view of his future.

By midwinter Mom's mental state had deteriorated so much that she ended up back in the hospital; now Diane's burden was even more overwhelming. Once again, however, Mom emerged from shock treatments less anxious and at least temporarily more able to get through life. Then that spring her condition suddenly improved rapidly, so that she seemed almost normal again.

Wells, our two daughters, and I had been living in Paris since the beginning of February on a sabbatical leave from his professorship. When we heard of Mom's rapid improvement, we invited her to join us for a couple of weeks in June. We were delighted to see how well she was and how much she enjoyed visiting Paris again.

Mom and I had long talks together about Kent, both of us seeing little hope in his situation as the months wore on and he continued to drink. She told me that Kent had discussed with her the possibility of suicide, saying he could drive his car off a mountain road. He had also laid his troubles at her door by telling her he had not asked to be born. Whether or not he committed suicide was his own business, but I was appalled that he had discussed his plans for it with Mom when the rest of us were trying so hard to help her get well. She believed the danger of suicide was real and had discussed the possibility with Dr. Galvin, almost coming to the point of seeing it as the only termination to a hopeless situation. We both feared that after all Diane had done for Kent, he might end it all in her basement. In the bright sunshine in the Tuileries Gardens, Mom and I sat together watching carefree children sail their boats on the pool while we talked of what horrible things might be taking place in that dismal basement on the other side of the world. I was especially apprehensive that Kent might decide to take his own life while Mom was away.

Through all our conversations, I tried to steer Mom into an acceptance of whatever the outcome would be and a realization that we were powerless to change Kent's destiny. I wanted her to strive for her own happiness and stability regardless of how he chose to live his life. She had always struggled valiantly against the vicissitudes of her life, maintaining a positive outlook in the face of innumerable difficulties, while Kent viewed the world in a very negative way.

When Mom left Paris, I felt relatively satisfied with her frame of mind and hoped she would not drag herself down again by trying to take care of Kent. At the end of the summer, however, she decided to rent a larger apartment to share with him, thus assuming the daily burden of cooking and caring for an alcoholic. By the time we had returned from Europe, this arrangement was a fait accompli. Diane had disapproved but had been powerless to stop it.

Things dragged along that fall with Kent still visiting Dr. Galvin, who was becoming increasingly disenchanted with him. Since more than a year had passed with no visible progress, Diane and I began to consider having Kent "take the cure." Diane consulted Dr. Galvin on this point, but he was not enthusiastic about the chances of success. He had come to the conclusion that Kent had a "character disorder" and said to Diane, "Your brother will end his life as an alcoholic." For want of a better solution, he suggested Mom and Diane consider city or state treatment facilities.

At this point I decided to write for advice to the National Council on Alcoholism. They replied that treatment by a psychiatrist is not nearly as effective for an alcoholic as treatment in a custodial situation where the patient is prevented from drinking. From their list of treatment centers, I found an excellent one in Minnesota that was called Hazelden, and Kent and the rest of the family agreed it would be worth trying. He left Denver in December and spent six months at the facility, much longer than their staff had anticipated. He later said they found him a difficult case. Previously he had announced that Dr. Galvin said he was one of the most difficult cases he had ever treated; this was almost a badge of honor in Kent's mind.

Treatment at Hazelden is built around the basic tenets of Alcoholics Anonymous, most of which Kent never accepted. Later he told us that the staff finally became annoyed with him because he sat in the group therapy sessions arguing with every point made, like the village agnostic. According to Kent, he and the members of the staff finally parted company because they were sick of each other. Ten years later he made this revealing statement: "Everyone at Hazelden kept telling me I would be able to handle the problems in my life if I would just stop drinking. I finally got so fed up with hearing that line I decided that I would not touch a drink for two years after I left just to prove to them that my life would still be no good."

Although they could not change his basic attitudes, Hazelden counselors did rehabilitate Kent and helped him reenter the workforce in a sheltered manner. When Kent left Hazelden early in the summer of 1972, he moved into a halfway house where reformed alcoholics lived together. After a few months living there and working in a furniture factory operated by Alcoholics Anonymous, he was able to reenter the data processing field. He held a job for a year in Minneapolis and then moved to Ohio, where he worked as a computer programmer for seven or eight years.

CHAPTER NINE

After Mom had recovered from her first mental collapse, Diane and I had felt almost the same joy we would have experienced had she been resurrected from the dead. Recoveries from subsequent breakdowns never again brought the same surge of hope because we could never escape the fear that it was only a matter of time until Mom would once again slip away from us into the painful darkness of mental illness. When Mom joined us in Estes Park in the summer of 1972, she was again having serious problems. She talked incessantly in a manic phase of manic-depression, which we soon realized was the most apt clinical description of her condition. Meal times were impossible, as we all listened to Mom's frenzied monologues from the beginning to the end of dinner. On the few occasions when outsiders were present, the situation was even more distressing and embarrassing. As long as we were in the house, there was no escaping the sound of her voice. Her behavior became erratic also. Awakened one night at 3 A.M. by noises in the kitchen, I found Mom busily waxing the kitchen chairs. When she was in a manic phase, she would also go on spending sprees. Luckily, she never bought more than several moderately priced items like an ice cream freezer, but she made these purchases with a reckless abandon uncharacteristic of her normal personality.

The situation would have been almost unbearable had Wells and I not escaped from the house occasionally to go on long hikes. After the constant emotional turmoil in the cabin, the silence of the mountains was a relief. Even then we carried Mom's difficulties with us, trying as we walked across the flower-strewn tundra to decide how we could handle what were beginning to seem like overwhelming and insoluble problems.

By the end of July, matters were approaching a crisis. To add to our problems, Mom's landlady called to say that Mom's apartment had been burglarized and her television stolen, so Mom decided to go down to Denver to check on the situation. Wells and I weren't free to go with her because we had some New England friends arriving to go hiking with us. Unfortunately, when Mom viewed the scene of the robbery, she became very upset and experienced such feelings of paranoia that she called up a couple of Diane's friends to tell them that the police were after them.

Just after Mom had gone to Denver, Dad unexpectedly showed up at Estes. Learning that she was in Denver in a deteriorating state, he drove down to bring her back to the cabin. When he saw how anxious and talkative she was, however, he decided it would be best to take her to a hotel downtown because our children were at the cabin. At the hotel, Dad soon realized what a problem he had on his hands. Mom wouldn't stop talking, even in the middle of the night. Fearing that she would disturb the other guests, he in desperation attempted to hold his hand over her mouth. Of course it didn't work. The rest of us would never have tried it even though we had often felt driven to that point after listening to Mom talk for endless hours.

When Dad saw the state of disarray of Mom's checkbooks the next morning, he became so concerned about her ability to manage her own affairs that he called me to say he had decided to take her back to Palisade to establish a conservatorship and guardianship over her. I at once objected that she shouldn't go back home in such a condition, and the issue was left unresolved.

When Dad called from the hotel, I was about to leave for the annual meeting of our homeowners association. I was relieved that Mom wasn't home, so I wouldn't be forced to tell her she couldn't go along. But to my great dismay, about halfway through the meeting she came in the door looking wild-eyed and disturbed. She made a strange comment or two at the meeting as I held my breath, expecting an embarrassing disaster at any moment, but fortunately no major problem occurred. At the end of the session, I quickly whisked her away, cursing Dad to myself for having driven her out to the meeting to expose herself to the neighbors in that sorry condition.

As I drove away with Mom saying one crazy thing after another, my mind was racing over possible courses of action. I couldn't take her back to the cabin to let my daughters see their grandmother in such a deplorable state. But the last thing I wanted to do was to turn her over to Dad and let him take her back to Palisade, 250 miles away from any good mental hospital.

To give myself time to maneuver, I suggested to Mom we go out for lunch. After ordering, I went outside to a phone booth. I called Mom's other psychiatrist, Dr. Merrill, who handled her case whenever she had to be hospitalized because Dr. Galvin was not affiliated with a hospital. I explained that Dad insisted upon taking Mom back to Nebraska, but Diane and I thought such a move would be disastrous. Although Dr. Merrill didn't think the return to Nebraska was a good idea either, he said, "After all, he's her husband, and I don't see how you can prevent him from taking her back there if he wants to do it."

That opinion couldn't have upset me more, but there was no way we could hospitalize her without Dr. Merrill's cooperation. I walked slowly back into the restaurant to face the impossible dilemma of what to do with Mom, whose behavior was becoming more extreme with every passing hour. After lunch I drove her downtown, where we met Dad in a parking lot on Main Street. Dad and I left Mom sitting in the car and sat on a bench by the river arguing the problem together. I said everything I could think of to try to convince him to take her to the hospital in Denver instead of taking her to Palisade, but he was adamant. And once Dad made up his mind about something, he was virtually immovable. It soon became clear there was no way I could stop him from driving off with her short of offering physical resistance or shouting for the police, both of which alternatives I considered and quickly discarded. Had we started a fight on Main Street, people might have thought the whole family was crazy.

So Dad drove off with Mom, who was totally out of her head by that point. Back at the cabin, I immediately called Helen Brown, the close family friend who had done house cleaning for Mom and Dad for years, and alerted her that Dad was on his way home with Mom and would probably arrive late that evening.

The next day all hell broke loose. We received a call from Helen, who told us that early that morning the neighbors had been awakened by the sounds of Mom screaming. She had broken the window in an upstairs bedroom, thrown her hair brush and shoes out onto the roof, and screamed for help. Of course, the whole town was soon in an uproar. As we pieced together the story, Dad and Mom had arrived in Palisade very late the preceding night. Mom later told me Dad had stopped along the way to help a couple of women change a tire, leaving her to swelter in the hot car. When they arrived in Palisade, Dad sent Mom upstairs by herself to sleep, but there were no screens upstairs, only storm sashes, so it was impossible to open any windows. To make matters worse, the upstairs was virtually an oven, as it was one of the hottest days in August. Mom told people she had broken the window because she was suffocating. For someone in her distressed condition, that extreme heat and lack of any ventilation must have been traumatizing.

In the midst of this crisis, Dad left Helen with Mom and drove off to McCook to talk to his doctor about the situation. Helen told us later that he was gone for five hours, leaving her all alone to take care of Mom in her wild state.

As soon as we were able to reach Dad by phone, we pleaded with him to send Mom back to the hospital in Denver in an ambulance. He refused to agree to that, however, and even mentioned taking her to the state mental hospital, a place of very limited resources. We were shocked to think he would suggest such a possibility because we feared she might never again get well if she were put in this state institution.

In desperation we called Dr. Galvin to let him know how bad things were. In an attempt to allay our concern, he made what has become a classic family statement often repeated as crisis followed crisis in the ensuing years: "Don't worry, the eleventh hour can't last forever!"

I made arrangements with the Denver hospital to be sure a bed was waiting if we could get Mom there. By the time we called Dad back, the strain was beginning to wear him down. Now, however, he said that if she had to go to the hospital, an ambulance was an unnecessary expense–he could put Mom in the back of one of the farm trucks. The image sickened us, as had the whole avoidable disaster.

Finally, I called an ambulance in McCook anyway and arranged to have it go up to Palisade, hoping that by the time it actually appeared, we could persuade Dad to let Mom go. As a last resort, I decided to try to pressure Dad via Mark, whom he loved very much. When I reached Mark in Canada and explained the problem, he agreed to call Dad right away and try to convince him to put Mom on the ambulance. Fortunately this plan worked, and we all were immensely relieved to receive a phone call from Helen saying Mom was at last safely on the way to Denver.

As Wells, Diane, and I discussed these painful events, we were furious to think that Dad was so insensitive that he would expose Mom to everyone in Palisade in an extreme state of mental collapse. She would have been absolutely mortified to know that people in Palisade had seen her in such a wild condition. Fortunately, she tended to forget what had happened during these extreme phases of her illness, but no one in Palisade ever forgot. Dad even left the window Mom had broken unrepaired for over two years, until I finally asked Helen Brown to have it fixed. As the window was located on the principal street leading downtown, it served as a constant reminder to every passerby that Audrey Krotter had been crazy.

Diane, Dad, and I now converged on Denver, where the struggle over Mom continued. When Dad announced that he was beginning legal action to get custody over her, Diane and I made clear our opposition and told him we were going to attempt to have Diane appointed guardian over Mom. In a bitter dispute in the lobby of Mom's hospital, Dad told us that he didn't want to see us again and that when he died, he didn't want us to come to his funeral. Diane and I located a lawyer at once and asked him to institute proceedings to have Diane appointed guardian over Mom. He said that a spouse usually took precedence in a case like this, so it was very important for us to obtain letters from all the children supporting the appointment of Diane as guardian.

Dad was so furious about the whole affair that he threatened to leave us none of his gold and silver if we persisted in opposing him. In spite of this threat, Diane, Mark, and I stood firm. After the latest Nebraska fiasco, it seemed unthinkable to abandon Mom to Dad's sole control.

I called to explain the situation to Kent, who was now living in a halfway house and working in a furniture factory. Since he had always loved Mom very much, I was sure he would write a letter of support. But to my dismay, he called back a day later to say that he had discussed the issue with Dad and had decided to remain neutral. After hanging up the phone, I burst into tears, so sharp was my sense of shock and betrayal at his words. More than any of us children, he had resented and criticized Dad for years, always faulting him for the way he treated Mom. Now when a choice was forced upon him, he didn't have the integrity to take a stand on her behalf but abandoned her to Dad in the hope of some day getting part of the gold and silver. The irony of it all was that Dad had already disinherited him and never changed his will, so his money still came to the rest of us.

Fortunately, the judge ruled in Diane's favor after Mom's psychiatrist testified that it would be much better for Mom to be under Diane's supervision. Mom herself was able to come into the hearing for a few minutes and request that Diane be appointed guardian instead of Dad.

During this hospitalization, Mom was successfully treated with lithium. In the course of his wide reading, Dad had run across an article about the successful use of this drug in treating mental problems. When I asked Dr. Merrill about lithium, he said it was mainly used for manic-depressives, and this was the first time he had seen Mom in a manic phase. He agreed it would be worth a try as an alternative to further shock treatments, and it was in fact quite miraculous what a sudden improvement lithium produced in Mom.

Once again we had to find a new living arrangement for Mom, and we decided a boarding situation would be best. Diane found a place where Mom stayed for several months, but after Christmas she began to slip again, and I could tell that Diane was understandably at the end of her rope trying to manage the situation. When she got really exhausted with the unremitting sequence of family crises, she would announce over the phone: "I'm sick and tired of trying to handle all these family problems. Some day I'm just going to take off for Alaska and not leave any address and that will be the last anyone hears from me." These days I was hearing a lot of Alaska talk, so I was becoming concerned.

Then one night I got a call from the young man who shared Diane's piano studio. He was worried that the strain of Mom's care was beginning to take its toll on Diane, who seemed so upset that he thought I should try to find some way to get Mom out of Denver. I had given him my number for just such an emergency, so I assured him I would do something quickly.

When Aunt Thelma heard that Mom was again having problems, she wanted to have her come to live with her in her California apartment. After a few months there, however, Mom again had to be hospitalized. She then lived for a year in a retirement hotel near my aunt's apartment. By the time Mom came out to Estes Park to spend the following summer with us, however, she had decided she didn't want to stay in California permanently. Knowing how much she enjoyed Estes Park, I suggested we might find her an apartment downtown. When she agreed to this idea, we looked around and found a nice place only a block from Main Street with beautiful views of the mountains. For the next four or five years, Mom lived in Estes Park, occasionally changing apartments and twice ending up back in the hospital for a short time.

CHAPTER TEN

After this exhausting sequence of family crises, we enjoyed a relatively quiet period for a few years. Kent was back in a steady programming job, and Mom's mental condition remained reasonably good. Mark married a Canadian medical student named Margaret Yates in 1973 and settled into law practice, acting as a public prosecutor. After an absence of seven years, Mark returned to spend a few days at Estes Park with Margaret one summer, and they seemed very happy together.

In the meantime, Dad had become quite restive living alone and had found himself a girlfriend named Eileen. She was much younger, probably in her early thirties, while Dad was now seventy. He wanted to buy Eileen a house in Palisade, but she didn't want to get that involved. I heard, however, that he paid over $20,000 for her to have open heart surgery. Dad himself told me that she continued a relationship with a man her own age during this period, and I suspect her relationship with Dad did not go beyond the platonic stage. When he took her on a cruise to Alaska, he rented separate cabins. He later told me that when he had related this fact to a physician friend, the latter had remarked, "That was a damn waste of money." At any rate, in the pictures from the trip he is absolutely beaming with pride to have Eileen at his side.

Eileen's reasons for entering a relationship with a seventy-year-old man may be open to question, but Dad's motivation clearly had many facets. His pride had been deeply hurt when Mom didn't return to Palisade; he felt he had been humiliated in the eyes of the town. Now he could in effect say to everyone, "See, this young woman finds me attractive!" When we came to visit him in Palisade during the summer, he talked a great deal about Eileen and also had her picture prominently displayed in the living room. In this photo from their Alaskan trip, she was dressed in a nineteenth-century barroom dancer's costume. My young daughters looked rather puzzled when Dad proudly pointed out the picture. I could see they were trying to figure out what their dignified grandfather's connection was with a woman who looked as if she belonged on a Western movie set.

Dad had been lonely during these years, and I'm sure he enjoyed Eileen's company very much. He irritated us all, however, by talking a lot about her to Mom, even going so far as to show Mom letters Eileen had written to him. He was probably trying to make her jealous, perhaps hoping he would get her to come home this way.

By the summer of 1976, Dad was pressuring Mom to give him a divorce. We were back in New England that summer because our third daughter was about to arrive, so I only became aware of this development through Diane. I was never sure whether Dad asked for his freedom because he had thoughts of remarriage or because he thought he could force Mom to return to Palisade in this way. Dr. Galvin, Diane, and I all thought Mom might as well give him the divorce since she had no intention of ever returning to Palisade. She refused to do so, however. I never discussed the subject with her, but I suspect she basically just didn't want to be a divorced woman. She may also have been trying to protect us children because she feared a new wife would divert much of Dad's money away from us.

During the following summer of 1977, when we were back in Estes Park, we learned from Kent that he was again having drinking problems. Ironically enough, at that same point Dad was beginning to reconsider his disinheritance of Kent, but when he heard Kent was again drinking, he decided to leave his will intact. From what Kent told us later, I think he had totally abstained during the first couple of years after he left Hazelden in 1972. Afterwards, I suppose he just gradually slipped again into a dependence on alcohol. Fortunately, he spent some time in a halfway house near his apartment, so he didn't immediately hit bottom and succeeded in holding his job a couple more years.

CHAPTER ELEVEN

In the fall of 1977, Wells and I left for England with our three daughters so that Wells could spend a sabbatical year at Cambridge University. We found a perfect house in the middle of an apple orchard near Cambridge and settled down to enjoy a peaceful year in the English countryside, far from my family's problems. In early October, however, we were awakened one morning by a phone call from Mom saying that Dad had had a massive heart attack and had collapsed on a street in San Francisco, where he was attending a conference on monetary policy. A passerby had given him mouth-to-mouth resuscitation because his heart was no longer beating. Although the doctors in a hospital emergency room had succeeded in reviving Dad, his heart had been stopped for so long that they feared brain damage had occurred, which was indeed the case.

Dad was in a coma for a couple of weeks, so I decided not to fly back to the States, given the great difficulty of either taking our twelve-month-old baby with me or leaving her with Wells. Diane was able to go to San Francisco briefly, and Mom was well enough at this point to stay in San Francisco to supervise Dad's care. At last Dad emerged from the coma, and the doctors then thought his survival chances were good, so it seemed best for me to stay in England unless his condition deteriorated. By early November, he had recovered sufficiently to be flown back to Denver, where he entered a nursing home because he was too weak and confused from brain damage to live by himself in Palisade.

Since business matters were now beginning to pile up in Nebraska, Diane decided she should get a conservatorship to handle Dad's affairs. Although I knew she had no talent at all for business, I saw no good alternative. Even if I had been at home that year, the court would probably have given precedence to a Colorado resident. Mark, as a Canadian citizen, was not a viable possibility, and of course Kent couldn't even manage his own affairs, let alone Dad's.

Thus it turned out that in December of 1977 Diane obtained a conservatorship in Colorado over Dad's property and a subsidiary conservatorship in Nebraska. At the time she obtained the conservatorships, we had no idea that Dad would live for several years and that Diane would have so much fateful power over the family wealth.

Dad's business property at this point consisted primarily of two lumberyards, which were left to coast along under their managers. For practical purposes, business matters were handled by Dad's first cousin, Gene Schroeder, a cattle breeder who lived in Palisade and was familiar with all Dad's business interests. Gene sent Diane the appropriate papers to sign when things needed to be done and oversaw the day-to-day operations himself.

To complicate matters, a local teenage boy broke into Dad's house while he was in the hospital and stole many of his gold and silver coins. Dad had become increasingly careless over the years about where he hid things. According to town rumor, this boy had boasted to a friend that he had watched Dad through a window and knew where he had hidden coins. Since he found a lot of them in the cedar chest in Dad's bedroom, he must have known where to look. Something apparently frightened him before he was finished because he left an overturned pail of coins on the back porch that Dad's caretaker, Clark Brown, discovered when he went over to the house to clean the furnace. A farmer south of town even found some foreign gold coins that had been thrown off the road onto his property. For all we know, there are still coins scattered through the weed-choked ditches along that country road. Of course, in a small town everyone knew who the thief was within a couple of days, but no one will ever know how much he got away with.

There was still more than enough hidden treasure for us to worry about in any case. For twenty years we had all speculated about what in the world we would do when Dad died or became incapacitated some day, leaving us to deal with his hoard of gold and silver. Despite our urging, we knew he had never made a list indicating where coins were hidden. We wondered if he even remembered all the places where he had squirreled things away over the years.

Now the time so long dreaded by us all had finally arrived; we had to locate all of Dad's hidden coins and move them safely to a bank. Wells and I decided we would have to cut short our travels in Europe that following summer and return to spend the month of August in Palisade gathering up the collection. We had also agreed with Diane that once we had combed through the south house property for gold and silver, we would then clear out all the rest of the furnishings and junk so that we could sell the south house. Dad's estate account had so little money in it that we had to raise what cash we could in this way. Wells and I had also decided to take Dad back to Palisade with us for the month of August because he had been begging to go home ever since he arrived in Denver. On one occasion he had escaped from the nursing home in his bathrobe in a futile attempt to get back to Palisade. When he saw two attendants coming to get him, he grabbed a light pole, but he was no match for two strong young men. Back to the nursing home they dragged him. If he wanted to go home that desperately, I thought we should let him spend at least a few weeks there, difficult as it would be to work around him and gather up his gold and silver without his noticing it.

The logistics of moving the hoard from Palisade to Denver presented enormous problems. Wells and I opted from the beginning for using an armored car, but Diane was adamantly opposed to that arrangement because it would be too public. I wasn't sure that was a disadvantage since I was concerned about how widespread the knowledge might be that Dad had been hiding away gold and silver coins for twenty years. If everyone in town knew an armored car had driven off with the gold and silver, there would be no incentive for anyone to break into the house and wreck it looking for coins, or worse yet, try to force any of us who happened to be there to tell them where they were hidden. We could be in some danger spending the month of August there if someone guessed we were hunting for a fortune in gold and silver.

Diane and I had to battle the issue via long distance telephone between Europe and Denver because all the arrangements had to be in place to move the collection almost immediately after our return to Palisade, so we could then bring Dad home. Diane's estate lawyer had proposed she hire an ex-FBI agent whom he knew to go out with a colleague to drive the coins back to a Denver bank, but I objected strongly to the risk involved. Since the shipment would not be insured, we would lose a fortune if the agent was robbed of the coins. (Those same coins in late January 1980 were worth $1.5 million.) Even a flat tire en route would have been a major disaster since the men would have had to unload by the roadside some one hundred small but heavy boxes of coins in order to change the tire.

I called Diane from telephones scattered all across France–from the post office of a tiny mountain village high in the Pyrenees, from the back room of a country grocery store near the Rhone River, and from a crowded telephone exchange trailer in the French Alps, where the callers on either side of me were speaking in Italian and French. It was enormously frustrating to be forced to resolve such a momentous issue under such communication difficulties, but I kept trying to convince Diane that it would be safer to use an armored car. Finally she found out from one of the armored car companies that they would not accept the shipment unless it were counted, bagged, and sealed by a bank. She thought this an insurmountable problem, but I saw no reason why a local bank could not handle the job. At last I gave up my objections to the FBI agent because I didn't see how else to resolve the question, given the deadlines facing us. Since our last phone call cost me $100, it wasn't practical to continue these trans-Atlantic arguments.

Wells and I and our three daughters, Marie, Kathryn, and Christine, who were eleven, eight, and not quite two, arrived back in Palisade at the end of July. It was an all too abrupt transition to leave the charm and beauty of Paris with its central axis of architectural splendor running from the Arc de Triomphe to Notre Dame and return to Palisade, Nebraska, with its dusty little Main Street where every other shabby building stood empty. There we found ourselves, however, and Diane joined us from Denver on the day of our arrival. That night after the children were asleep, we made plans for the treasure hunt the next morning. Our friends Helen and Clark Brown had offered to help this month in any way they could and began by inviting the children to spend the day with them while we searched for coins. They were still young enough that we wanted them to know nothing about the hidden treasure. Otherwise, they might have thought that although money doesn't grow on trees, one could find it lying about almost anywhere else.

Helen and Clark knew all about the gold and silver since Helen had dusted around it during all the years she had housecleaned for Mom and Dad. Our family had always relied totally upon the Browns' integrity, knowing they would never touch a single coin, although they lived on a very meager income from Clark's work at the Krotter gravel pit and

Helen's housework. Helen told me that she had once scolded Dad when she went over to the house to clean and found $10,000 spread out on his bed. She feared that such behavior might some day put her in an awkward position if money were ever missing. We decided to start our search at the south house. For many years the family had known that Dad had hidden gold coins in some sort of an old, unused heating duct located in a tiny storeroom near the furnace. Wells, Diane, and I drove out to the house with a sense of high adventure mixed with apprehension, not knowing whether thieves had already found the coins. A neighbor boy had broken into the south house a few months before, but as far as we knew, this thief had only taken a few objects of little value.

After we got out of the car, we stood for a moment in the weed-filled driveway, looking at the house where Diane and I had grown up, now sunk into a sorry state of decay. It had not been painted since my parents moved out some twenty years before, and an upstairs window was broken. Through the jagged hole fluttered a tattered curtain. The large picture windows Mom had been so proud of were pockmarked by bullet holes from the rifle of some joy-riding teenager. Since the back steps were about to collapse, we walked through the weeds to the front of the house. It gave us a strange feeling to survey the abandoned house with its paint peeling off and realize that it probably contained a fortune in gold and silver. When we entered the front door, we saw that the living room was piled with stacks of books so high they were toppling over. In the middle of the rug was a pile of plaster that had fallen from the ceiling, covering many of the books with jagged shards and white powder. We stepped around the dusty mess and headed for the basement.

With a feeling of great excitement, we went down the stairs and looked around the walls of the little storeroom, but we saw nothing that appeared to be the heating duct Mom had mentioned. We decided to go upstairs to the spot directly above the storeroom, where there was a large cold air duct in the floor. But this duct did not look promising when we opened it up, so we then looked into a hot air radiator nearby. This too proved fruitless. Feeling increasingly uneasy, we headed back down to the basement. This time we looked more carefully at the floor of the storeroom and discovered that a large pile of magazines concealed an opening leading down under the floor. When Wells reached down into the hole, he pulled out a couple of bags of gold coins. It was an immense relief to know that the coins had not all disappeared. This cache had an interesting history because Dad had originally told no one of its existence. During the Christmas vacation of 1958, he had walked out to the south house to fix the coal furnace one night. When two hours passed with no sign of Dad, Kent went out to check up on him and discovered he had had a heart attack. Dad later told Mom about the absolute panic that had gripped him when he realized he might die before he had a chance to tell anyone in the family about the gold coins hidden under the floor of the storeroom. It's a wonder the added stress didn't finish him off on the spot. While he was recovering in the hospital, he told Mom about this cache and also where he had hidden other coins.

Wells, Diane, and I next turned our attention elsewhere in the basement. The search was very exciting, yet at the same time we were frightened that someone might be waiting to rob us of the gold and silver once we located it. After all, the whole town knew that one thief had already found a large number of coins. For all we knew, that young man had boasted to other criminals in the state penitentiary that he knew where a hoard of gold and silver was hidden. But despite our apprehension, we had to keep looking, so we next investigated an old "fruit room" where we used to store canned goods. Mixed in with boxes of musty old teddy bears and other discarded toys tossed away here years ago, we found more coins. The bottom of an old clothes chute yielded a couple of large bags of quarters. Next we decided to check the attic, since Mom had always thought Dad had hidden things there. Sure enough, when Wells climbed up through the linen closet shelves into the attic, he found many more bags of coins. The treasure hunt was off to a great start, but we had only begun.

After spending the morning checking out the most logical spots in the south house, we went back into town for lunch, carrying along all of our loot. We now had to find places in the town house to hide all the coins so that our children wouldn't see them. All month long we had to keep up the same dual game of hide and seek, finding gold and silver and then hiding it all again.

We had decided to dig in the garage that afternoon for the large cache Dad had buried there. There was a logistics problem involved in this operation, however, because it would look suspicious if anyone saw us carrying shovels out to the garage. We finally settled on the following plan: I went out in the backyard to see that the coast was clear, and then Wells carried the shovels out and concealed them in the tall weeds by the garage door opening onto the alley. Fifteen minutes later we went out again, and seeing no one in sight, we unlocked the garage and slipped in with the shovels.

The garage space was large, perhaps 40' by 60', but I had a vague impression where the coins were buried from my earlier conversations with Dad. I thought that from the southwest corner we should come twice as far along the length of the room as along the width. From Mom's information that Dad had moved a heavy table to conceal the spot, we decided we should look first under the long table in the middle of the room. We poked around under it with the shovels, but it did not appear that the ground there had ever been disturbed. The measurements I had in mind did not correspond with the position of the table either. Concluding it was possible that someone had moved the table during the intervening decade, we started investigating elsewhere. We were beginning to fear we would have to dig up half of the huge garage when Wells suddenly found a spot where it seemed easier to dig. After going down about a foot, he exclaimed in great excitement, "I've hit something; there's wood down here!" A few more shovelfuls revealed what appeared to be the top of a very large wooden box. Wells began digging faster now that he thought he had found the buried treasure. In that closed space, the air quickly filled with dust that soon became so thick we had to step outside for a few minutes to breathe some fresh air and let the dust settle. Eventually the whole top of the box was exposed; it was about 2' by 4' in size. After we had pried off the lid, we saw the box was about two feet deep and was filled with bags of coins. When Wells reached down to pull up a bag so we could open it, the bottom of the bag fell out because the canvas had rotted during the ten years it had lain in the ground. Shiny dimes spilled out in every direction into the box and the surrounding dirt.

It was obvious that we had to transfer everything into different containers, so I went back into the house to see what I could find. My search yielded several coffee cans and lots of old half-gallon milk cartons that Dad had kept in an old clothes chute, probably for future coin storage. Since a small box of coins about 8" square by 6" deep weighs about ten pounds, we had to use small containers for convenience in handling. The whole operation presented major difficulties because each bag we lifted broke, rolling coins back down into the box. As we worked, dirt slipped down the sides of the hole into the box, so we had to pick up handfuls of coins, shake out as much dirt as possible, and then put them into all the odd containers. We had to work very carefully, lowering handfuls of coins gently into the cans and boxes so that the jingle of coins could not be heard in the alley outside. But we also had to work quickly. In just a day or two the agents were coming to pick everything up, and there were still many places left to investigate. As it was, it took us several hours to get all the coins out of the box and into containers. Then we had to make trip after trip across the backyard and into the house, carrying the coins.

Over the course of our handling of the hoard, we became adept at carrying two or three little boxes weighing some thirty pounds and making it appear effortless. Caution was essential because we faced the constant risk that a curious neighbor or passerby might be observing our actions. At best they would have been very puzzled at the unusual activity; at worst, given my father's reputation for hoarding coins, it could have been immediately obvious what was going on.

When Wells and I were finally through emptying the box, which turned out to contain only silver coins, we filled in the hole and dragged some junk over the spot to conceal it. Then we looked around the room a while, testing various spots to see if there was any sign that anything else had ever been buried. Finally we had to give up since the room was too large for us to dig everywhere. A metal detector would have been useless because hundreds of old nails and other small pieces of metal had become embedded in the dirt over the years.

It was a curious feeling to have discovered and dug up all that money. For some reason, ever since I was a child I have had recurring dreams that I am digging in the earth and discover coins. I suspect this is a fairly common dream, although Wells never has such dreams and says it's in the genes. When we first found the buried coins that day, we were elated. Then as we transferred handful after handful of coins, becoming dirtier and dirtier with the brown dust from the earth and the black dust of the silver, an odd feeling of revulsion began to set in, and we started to feel bored and exhausted with the whole operation. In fact, it soon became a joke among Wells, Diane, and me that one of us would go off looking somewhere and come back saying, "Bad news, I found more coins!"

After we had finished the garage operation, we began to check various places around the town house. Since we knew Dad had once hidden coins in the attic, I stuck my head up through the entrance to look around. Seeing nothing, I concluded that he had long ago transferred these coins into the garage cache. We next surveyed the kitchen and decided to check the top shelves of the cupboards, which were built-in from the floor to the ten-foot-high ceiling. Wells climbed up on a high stool to open the doors. At first glance the cupboards appeared to be full of Limited Edition Club books in their familiar red wrappers. When he pulled out a few boxes of books, however, he discovered that behind them were bags and bags of coins. There was such a tremendous weight on the top shelf it was amazing it had never collapsed. Off the kitchen was a large pantry lined with cupboards, where we found still more coins concealed among the cans of food.

Another major operation was to check all the bookshelves in the upstairs and downstairs libraries. This was no small task because Dad owned thousands of volumes. On one occasion years earlier, Aunt Thelma had decided to dust some books in the upstairs library. To her amazement, she discovered a few gold coins hidden behind a book. Thus we had to check every shelf. It was a blessing that paper money was anathema to Dad, or we would have had to check 11,000 books to see if bills were hidden between the pages. In the downstairs library, the books were two rows deep on every shelf. Clear up on top of the book cases, eight feet from the floor, were stored several sets of encyclopedias. Dad had decided that some of the old editions of the Encyclopedia Britannica had more information about certain subjects. Hence he had bought three sets of Encyclopedia Britannica from the 1920s to supplement his more recent set. This was the kind of purchase that had driven Mom to distraction, if not out of her mind.

Diane and Wells also hastily checked the drawers forming the bottom three feet of each bookshelf and found many coins there. A couple of weeks later I sorted more carefully through all those large drawers, numbering thirty-six in all. While looking for hidden coins among all the old newspapers, letters, and magazines, I found a considerable number of $20 gold pieces scattered randomly about, sometimes in boxes, sometimes only in envelopes. Each was then worth about $500.

As I picked up one letter and was about to throw it away without opening it, I noticed that it felt slightly heavy. Sure enough, Dad had ordered a couple of Krugerrand gold coins from a friend, who had enclosed them with a letter. I had almost thrown a thousand dollars in the trash. Years later when the bookshelves were finally dismantled and moved out of the house, the drawers yielded five more gold coins.

By the time night approached on that first day, we had consolidated so much gold and silver into the town house that we felt extremely apprehensive, knowing that we had coins worth hundreds of thousands of dollars in the house, yet not knowing whether anyone had been carefully watching our movements that day. Police protection in our tiny town was minimal; Palisade had one town marshal, who held the job in addition to his regular employment. The county sheriff was thirty minutes away, and we had no weapons in the house.

As Wells and I were lying in bed about midnight, trying to fall asleep in the sweltering heat, we heard a noise in the yard below our second-story bedroom. Suddenly alert and tense, we listened to the further sounds of movement that were clearly audible through the open windows. I was on the outside of the bed, so I crept silently over to the window to see if I could see something. There in the side yard below I saw a figure moving about, and a feeling of terror swept over me that we were about to be robbed and murdered. Our baby lay peacefully sleeping in her crib only two feet away, her quiet breathing mingling with the ominous sounds from the yard below that I was straining to hear. Suddenly I thought how ironic it would be if we all died in our attempt to get the gold and silver. For all we knew, someone had been waiting for us to arrive in Palisade and locate all the coins. All at once we were startled by a whistle from across the street. Looking that direction, I saw two teenage boys dart across the alley. Then the person in the yard beneath our windows ran across the street to join them. The terror that had gripped me eased somewhat as I realized that these might just be teenagers running around. Perhaps no one was going to murder us in our beds after all. We immediately called the town marshal, who drove around the neighborhood, but found no one, so we finally fell into an uneasy sleep.

When morning returned, with a Nebraska sun of August so intense it was almost blinding, we put our nighttime fears behind us and continued our search. In the south house, we found a large metal box of brilliant uncirculated silver dollars in an upstairs closet. In the town house we found a similar metal box of dollars in the far recess of the coat closet located under the staircase. As usual, we had to move away a ton of junk to reach the silver. Once again Dad had been protected against burglars by the sheer enormity of his accumulation of random possessions.

Coins kept turning up in the most unexpected places. One day when I was talking on the phone, I happened to look down at a small shelf nearby and there I saw a little box sticking out from behind some books. When I hung up the phone and opened the box, sure enough, it was full of quarters. Discoveries like this made it very apparent that we would not find all the coins until we had cleaned out every building Dad owned from top to bottom, but at least we could now send off the bulk of the hoard to Denver.

As the pile containing boxes and bags and cans of coins became ever larger, we kept reporting to the FBI agent in Denver so that he could decide what sort of vehicles he and his colleague should bring. Soon it was obvious that one of them should rent a van. In order to give them an idea of the weight involved, we weighed everything we had collected, box by box and can by can, using a bathroom scale. To our amazement, we discovered we had a total of two tons of gold and silver coins.

Our plan was to have the agents drive out to Nebraska on the eve of the day we intended to ship so that they could load everything up early one morning and depart before their activity excited the town gossips. We considered the possibility of loading in the middle of the night but decided that would excite too much suspicion if anyone did happen to see us. After carefully observing the early morning pattern of the town, we decided it would be best to start loading at 6 A.M. before many people were on the streets.

On the afternoon of the agents' scheduled arrival, they called us from the nearby town of Imperial, where we had agreed they would rent a motel room. Coincidentally enough, they had booked a room at the Golden West Motel. We arranged for them to drive to Palisade that afternoon to look at the collection and make plans for loading it the next morning. We sent Marie and Kathryn over to the Browns' to stay all night so they would be out of the way, but Christine stayed home with us since she couldn't talk enough to tell anyone what she was seeing. That afternoon, as we were hastily trying to collect all the boxes of coins we had hidden away out of sight of our older girls, we ended up with Christine underfoot in all the confusion. She soon discovered it was fun to scoop up handfuls of coins, and she started saying "Mo-ey, mo-ey," as the coins slipped through her tiny fingers. It was the understatement of the summer. When the agents arrived, they were astonished to see the extent of the hoard, as we uncovered box after box. They both were full of questions about where we had found it all and what kind of a person Dad was.

As luck would have it, it poured rain the next morning, a rare occurrence in southwest Nebraska. The downpour helped keep people off the streets but made it harder for Wells and the agents to load the van and car. While Diane and I stacked the boxes of coins on the back porch, they made dozens of trips to the van, each carrying two or three very small but very heavy boxes. Anyone watching could not have helped but wonder why these men were going endlessly back and forth with such small loads.

When everything was at last ready, they drove off. Diane rode with the agent in the van because she had to be in Denver to sign everything into the huge vaults she had rented. I thought she was courageous to make the trip; I would not have wanted to do so. The agents were all prepared for any problems with sidearms and two-way radio communication. When we saw how old the rented van was, we were especially concerned that it might break down on the way. It had also occurred to me that if these agents were not honest, they could arrange to be "robbed" on an almost deserted area of the highway winding across the plains and share the loot with an accomplice. The trip across the arid Colorado plains was uneventful, however, and we were greatly relieved to receive a call from Diane late that afternoon reporting that the gold and silver was all safe at last in the bank vaults.

Helen Brown reported that the only mention she ever heard of the operation was at her bridge club that afternoon, when one of the women asked, "What was going on over at the Krotters' this morning? I saw some men loading a van." Helen had our cover story all ready and said, "Oh, the girls were lucky and found a book dealer to buy a lot of the extra books." To this day, it seems incredible that we could have dug up and ferreted out two tons of silver and gold coins and moved them out of that sleepy little town without anyone noticing.

CHAPTER TWELVE

With the collection gone, we were free at last to bring Dad home. We drove to Estes Park to spend the night with Mom and Diane and then picked up Dad in Denver. When I walked into his room at the nursing home, I was shocked to see how frail he was after his long illness. I had last seen him as a vigorous man who moved quickly down a street or across a room. Now he had become an old man who shuffled as he walked and spoke with slurred diction.

Dad couldn't wait to get home and was delighted when we got him back to Palisade. But as a result of his brain damage, he had forgotten many things. He walked over to a small bookcase in the living room holding no more than sixty books and said, "Where did all of these books come from? I didn't know I owned that many books!" Considering he actually owned 11,000 volumes, that was quite a memory lapse. Oddly enough, for a man whose monomania for twenty years had been to amass as many gold and silver coins as possible, he had also forgotten the enormous size of his hoard and had only vague memories of the collection. He obviously thought of it as just a few hundred coins, although the number of nickels alone was over 200,000. Finding a couple of rolls of silver nickels in his office one day, he sat in his chair all that evening, picking up the nickels one by one and studying them carefully. Over and over he counted them, obviously perplexed by their presence. It was clear that he sensed these coins were important to his life, but could not remember why. Then one day as we walked by the garage he said in a loud voice, "That's where I buried my coins." Thank heavens no one else was on the street at the time.

Fortunately, Dad was so happy to be back in Nebraska that he was content just to sit in his easy chair and read all day long. This left us free to concentrate upon our other main objective for the month, which was to clean out the south house property and sell it, a huge task because of the many buildings involved. In addition to the main house, there were two small garages, a large double garage, a sprawling old chicken house that had been converted into a recreation room, my grandparents' little house, a hog house, a large barn, and a storm cellar. Almost all of these buildings were jammed full of newspapers, books, furniture, old cars, and just plain junk.

Downtown we also had overwhelming problems. The town house contained eleven large rooms with many closets and bureaus that we had to check for valuables. The basement was piled so high you could barely walk through it. And we didn't even dare toss out a box of old newspapers without picking through them one by one to see if coins were concealed between the pages.

What made our task seem almost impossible was that Dad also owned eight large buildings on Main Street. To Mom's dismay, he had been gradually buying up these buildings because they seemed such a bargain. He couldn't resist buying the old movie theater, for example, when it came on the market for only $2,000. The price seemed to Dad a steal for a large brick building like that. All these eight buildings were theoretically vacant, but they were actually full of junk. These unused buildings had made it much too easy for Dad to save everything that passed through his hands.

One of the first nights after our arrival in Palisade, I went over to Main Street and looked through the old hardware building. The main part of the first floor was covered with hardware stock that Dad had just left sitting there when he closed down the hardware ten years earlier. In the back room was furniture that had been moved over from the town house when Mom redecorated. Down in the basement were stacks and stacks of dusty old business records, unwanted articles of merchandise, and all sorts of discarded objects that had been deposited there to save carting them to the dump. I walked slowly around the store, thinking about the other seven large buildings on Main Street all full of things to be sorted. At midnight I went home, physically exhausted from the day's work and mentally overwhelmed by the nightmare vision of all those buildings full of piles of things to be sorted and gotten rid of. As I thought about all we had to clean up in the next few weeks, I hardly had the courage to face a job that seemed virtually impossible. Mom's frequent references to cleaning the Augean stables all too aptly described the undertaking.

There were not enough hours in the day for all we had to accomplish. Every morning we got up at seven o'clock, had a quick breakfast, and started to work. We were usually still working after ten o'clock at night and fell into bed exhausted shortly before midnight. With the temperature rising to the mid-90s every day and often hitting 100 degrees, we were quickly worn out carrying heavy loads up and down stairs and heaving them onto the truck.

When we first arrived, it was obvious there were many things to be thrown away, so I bought a case containing a dozen boxes of large garbage bags. It seemed ironic that since Dad had always bought items in case lots, I now had to buy garbage bags by the case to clean up after him. It quickly became apparent, however, that the job would require more than several dozen garbage bags. We had to borrow a large dump truck and by the time we finished cleaning out the Main Street buildings the following summer, we had filled the truck twenty-seven times. It seemed unbelievable that one man could have bought and stored so many things he didn't really use or need.

When we started cleaning out the south house property, we could see that although things like stacks of newspapers should go directly to the dump, there was an enormous amount of furniture, dishes, and other household goods that would have to be sold in some way. Distasteful as the idea of holding a public sale was to us, it soon became obvious that an auction was the only way to move everything out quickly at reasonable prices, so we scheduled one for the end of August.

Although we failed to find further coins in the south property, we did run across some strange things. Among all the newspapers in the double garage, we found an unopened box containing a thousand stamped envelopes with Dad's return address printed on them. The postage was three cents, which rather dated them. When we took them in to the postmaster to claim our $30, he said, "Why, I'd save those; they're so old they must be worth something!" Since this kind of thinking had got us into our present mess, we settled for the $30.

The south house had been in a strange state of limbo during the past twenty years. My parents left it in 1957 to move downtown for the winter and never returned. For years Mom continued to do the laundry at the south house because Dad told her it was too complicated to install the washing equipment in the town house. Everything had been left in place at the south house for the past twenty years. We even found vanilla and sugar still sitting on the kitchen shelves. To our amazement, the large chest freezer in the basement was still plugged in and running, typical of the sheer waste involved in letting a house stand unused for that many years. We even found bags of old cookies in the freezer, but had no desire to sample a twenty-year-old cookie. Dad had also kept the coal furnace running all those years to avoid draining the pipes. Even before the energy crisis, it was a frivolous use of resources.

Since we had no idea where coins might be hidden away, we couldn't just hire people to help us clear things out. Only Clark and Helen Brown knew about the coins, so they did everything they could to help us evenings and weekends. They had worked for a lifetime for the Krotters at low wages, and now we felt that we were once again taking advantage of their kindness and devotion. Clark even rescued Christine one day when she managed to get out the screen door when no one was looking and toddled down to Main Street, where Clark saw her in the middle of the street as he was driving along in his pickup. Fortunately, only an occasional car drove down Main Street.

All month long we left the house early in the morning, came back at noon for lunch, dirty and exhausted, disappeared again for the afternoon, and returned for supper even more covered with grime. Dad was still rather disoriented and confused about what was going on around him. He occasionally looked up from his book and asked, "What are you doing today?" or "Where are you going?" but fortunately settled for our evasive answers. One day, however, he startled us by saying he would take us out to the south house the next morning to show us where he had hidden some gold and silver. Of course we were worried how we could possibly explain why the coins had all vanished. Fortunately, when morning came, he said nothing more about it. This was typical of his mental condition during that first year after his heart attack; memories would suddenly surface and then sink once more into oblivion.

After we had finished cleaning out the south house property, we decided to tackle the basement of the town house. It was piled five feet deep everywhere with stacks of newspapers, magazines, boxes of old junk mail, and other trash. Only a narrow path led through the clutter to the furnace room. All sorts of strange objects were mixed in with the publications. A large garbage can was full of repulsive-looking black things the size of a small apple. I looked at them in horror, wondering if they were ancient decayed potatoes, but discovered they were only black walnuts still in their original outer covering.

We had reason to be particularly careful sorting through the basement. When Diane had made a trip to Palisade after the robbery that winter, she had taken all the gold coins she could find in the library drawers and hidden them in various spots in the basement, making herself a little map. She had missed one box when we had gathered up everything to ship to Denver, and while we were sorting through a carton of coal-dust-covered newspapers, we suddenly discovered it.

By late afternoon we had worked our way over to the far room beyond the furnace room. This was the final resting place of the cases of orange marmalade. By now the marmalade was a dozen years old and had turned a dark color, so we could hardly add the cases to the auction. Time was running short that afternoon, so we decided to leave the marmalade there and use what time remained to sort other shelves where we might find more coins or at least antiques for the auction.

We also had another possible hiding place to check out in the basement. A friend of Dad's from McCook had contacted us to say that Dad had discussed with him the possibility of breaking up the concrete floor in his basement to bury more gold or silver. Thus the friend urged us to look very carefully at the basement floors in both the town house and the south house to see if any spot appeared to have been recemented. We checked all the floor surfaces that we could, and Wells was even able to check the floor of the coal bin in the south house since there wasn't too much coal left in it. The town house coal bin was more of a problem because it still contained a lot of coal, so we were not able to check out the floor at that point.

A few years later when I went out to Palisade after my parents had died to clear out the town house so that we could sell it, I decided to ask a young cousin to shovel the coal around from one side of the large coal bin to the other so we could see if the cement floor had ever been disturbed. My cousin Linda, who still lived in southwest Nebraska, brought her son Bradley over to do the shoveling. My cousin Fred also showed up for the occasion. So here we were, four Krotter cousins standing in the coal bin when suddenly the door opened and there stood my cousin Gene Schroeder and an appraiser named Bob Horn, whom he was showing through the house. How were we to explain what four Krotters were doing in the coal bin? We didn't even try. Bob had probably heard enough rumors about Dad's collection that he figured it out for himself.

We realized when we sold the houses and other buildings we still owned in Palisade that we might not have found all the gold and silver Dad had hidden away. At least, according to Nebraska's "buried treasure law," any treasure that is found on property that has been sold belongs to the estate of the person who hid it, not to the finder. Nevertheless, if more gold and silver is ever found on property Dad owned, I would be happy to give twenty percent of my share to the finder.

CHAPTER THIRTEEN

Dad was the ultimate pack rat, whether he was gathering up gold and silver or newspapers and furniture and books. Everywhere we looked we discovered more and more things to add to the auction. By the time we searched the Main Street buildings, cleared out the south house property, and gleaned excess furniture from the town house, we had found hundreds of pieces of furniture to sell. Tucked away in the corners of closets or store rooms were countless odd things. One box held twenty glass candy dishes, another, a dozen screwdriver sets. Many of these items appeared to be purchases Dad had made at close-out sales of other stores. It was never clear why he bought these things; he just put them away in an unused building and forgot about them. Some objects had definite sale value, but others were clearly white elephants. We found at least half a dozen new orange juice squeezers of the type operated by a lever. Dad always loved these squeezers, and, as usual, he hadn't stopped with buying just one. One day we discovered a small box under the brass bed that was so heavy we were sure it contained coins. But there in the box lay two more orange juice squeezers.

Thus far we had succeeded in keeping Dad unaware of the coming auction. We knew he would be furious to see us selling any of his possessions, but we had little choice at this point since we needed large sums of cash to pay off pressing estate debts. Only a few months earlier, Wells and I had been forced to lend the estate $8,000 to pay Dad's nursing home bill. The money we so urgently needed could best be raised by selling off the south house property and its contents. We had explained our reasons for holding the auction to Mom, who had reluctantly agreed to this course of action. There was obviously no way to discuss this decision with Dad, so we had to get him out of town for a couple of days while we held the auction. After some thought, I suggested he go to the hospital in Imperial for a day or two to have some tests done. This plan worked so well he didn't find out about the auction until a year later. I drove him to Imperial the day before the auction. Early that afternoon I returned to Palisade, greatly relieved to have Dad safely out of the way. We had worked so hard shifting a mountain of his possessions that we couldn't wait to get rid of everything at the auction the next day. The auctioneers had assured us that by sundown everything would be gone, as though vultures had picked the place clean.

Diane had decided to return from Estes Park for the auction because many old friends would be there. Shortly after she arrived that afternoon, she announced, "I've got some bad news for you; Mom is coming home for the auction. She'll be arriving on the midnight bus." I was absolutely stunned by her words. I had just managed with great effort and ingenuity to get Dad out of the way, and now Mom was about to descend upon us. Since her mental condition had deteriorated sharply during the last couple of weeks, the auction was the last place she belonged. Diane claimed she had been unable to stop her from coming, but it was obvious that with a little imagination she could have kept Mom from making the trip back to Nebraska. Diane had arranged for Kent, who was visiting at Estes Park, to drive Mom to the bus. He could have used car trouble or any number of ruses to avoid arriving at the bus on time. It's not that hard to outwit someone who is out of their mind. As a last resort, Diane could have just stayed at Estes Park with Mom. I was furious that she had not at least called to let me know Mom's intentions so that I could have found a way to stop her. After the long weeks of horrendous labor we had spent preparing for the auction, it looked as if all our efforts might achieve nothing. If Mom appeared at the sale in an irrational state or worse yet, if she publicly objected to the proceedings, everyone would be so reluctant to bid that the whole auction could grind to a halt, with great embarrassment to all of us.

Wells and I tried desperately to think of a way to avert this disaster headed toward us on the midnight bus. We were especially concerned to shield our daughters from the situation because we wanted to keep them unaware of their grandmother's history of mental illness until they were a little older. And we couldn't let Mom expose herself to her former friends and neighbors in her present condition.

Without having reached any solution, Diane and I drove out to the highway to meet the midnight bus. When we picked Mom up, she was in bad shape. To play for time, I drove back to the house and said, "Let's just sit here in the driveway for a while and talk." As we listened to Mom ramble on and on, nothing could have been more obvious than that she was completely out of her head. While she was raving, I kept turning over in my mind the various alternatives open to us. If I took her into the house, the children would carry that terrible memory of their grandmother through life. She clearly could not be in Palisade during the auction; her mental condition was as bad as I had ever seen it. Nothing was more essential than to get her out of town as fast as possible in an ambulance headed to the hospital in Denver.

By now it was about 12:30 A.M., and the urgent problem was where to spend the night, or at least the intervening hours until we could put Mom on an ambulance. We couldn't go out to the south house. There wasn't even any running water there, and in just a few hours, when dawn arrived, the men would be moving everything out into the yard for the auction. I went over a mental list of friends and relatives, trying to think of somewhere we could spend the night. The best possibility seemed to be the home of my cousin Chuck Schroeder. It was relatively isolated on a farm outside of town, and his wife and he did not yet have children. So out we went, arriving shortly before 1 A.M. As I drove into the farmyard, their watchdog barked ferociously. I honked the horn, and before long a light went on in the upstairs window. My cousin leaned out to investigate the commotion, and seeing who it was, he came down to let us in. After I explained the bizarre situation as best I could, he readily agreed to let us spend the night in his living room.

Mom lay down on the couch but stayed awake all night. Diane and I stretched out on the rug, but it was impossible to fall asleep with the strident tones of Mom's incessant raving filling the room. Through the long hours of the night, we were forced to listen to the mother we had always adored slip further and further into an animal state of irrationality, all the while saying horrible things about us. Her face was so distorted that only a mindless hate radiated from her eyes. Over and over, she asserted that the lithium she had been taking was poisoning her. She was paranoid about both her doctors and her family and insisted we were all conspiring to kill her. Whenever she decided to stop taking lithium, as she had on this occasion, she ended up out of her mind in a short while. There was a certain risk in taking lithium, but she was not sane without it, so there was little choice but for her to use it. As it was, she survived twelve years on lithium.

As soon as I could slip away from Mom, I went into Chuck's study and called the hospital in Denver to be sure there was a bed available for her. The next problem was the ambulance. If I called the Palisade service, the news would soon spread all around town, so I first tried other communities. But everyone said they could not send their ambulance to serve a community that had its own. In desperation I gave up and dialed the Palisade number. The school superintendent answered in a sleepy voice and said Palisade's ambulance was already out-of-town. When I called back to McCook with this information, they agreed to send one at 6 A.M.

When it was beginning to get light at 5 A.M., I left Diane to put Mom on the ambulance and went back to town. Since Wells had not even known where we were all night, he was very relieved to see me. We had a quick breakfast and headed out to the south house, where Wells and some other men were going to move all the furniture outside. Only the day before, I had been eagerly looking forward to the auction as the climax of all our hard work and a chance to see many old friends who would be returning to Palisade for the occasion. Now I had to drag myself through the long and exhausting day, having had no sleep at all during an extremely stress-filled night. And underlying my dull weariness was a seething anger at Diane, an anger only heightened by her refusal to say anything about her role in precipitating this crisis other than "I'm not going to apologize for it; I've just been on overload this year."

The auction started at the south house at 9 A.M. Cars filled the field beside the house and lined the road all the way to town. A large crowd had come for the day, both to buy and to satisfy their curiosity, sensing it was the end of the Krotter era in Palisade. We were surprised to see what good prices things brought. Objects I would have called junk were considered "collectors' items."

That afternoon the auction moved downtown to the lumberyard, where we had been assembling the furniture and everything else we had found in the town buildings. Main Street was lined from one end to the other with cars; there had not been that many cars on Main Street since the lively Saturday nights of the late 1940s. Our auctioneers wore white cowboy hats and auctioned in a cowboy accent and style, very efficiently getting the best possible price for everything. The head auctioneer had sold off one orange juice squeezer and a few minutes later came to a box containing five others. As he opened it up, he said, "Well, folks, look at that–five more orange juice squeezers. These would make dandy Christmas gifts. Buy them now and solve your shopping problems!" I had thought he would have to give them away, but he got $5 a piece for them.

By 5 o'clock the auctioneers had sold everything and we had cleared $13,000. It was hard to believe that all the buildings of the south property were now empty. As we walked through the town house, however, Wells remarked, "Do you realize your father has so much stuff, we've been selling things all day long, and you can't tell the difference. The house is still cluttered!"

Only three days remained for us to finish up our business and prepare the town house for the winter. One of our last projects was to check the attic again since Dad had just told us that he had hidden a box of coins in a corner up there. We were surprised to hear this because we had already stuck our heads up through the attic opening and seen nothing. Now when I looked again more carefully, I saw a half-visible box, right where Dad had said it was. Since we had to enter the attic through an opening in the ceiling of the closet located in the girls' bedroom, we had to find a time to move the coins when they were gone and Dad was otherwise occupied, no small task.

The evening after the auction we saw our chance. Marie and Kathryn had gone off to a softball game, and an old friend of Dad's dropped by to visit with him. Wells and I excused ourselves from the living room and went upstairs to the attic entrance. We decided I would go up into the attic and hand the coins down to Wells, standing on a stool below. It turned out to be very hot and exhausting work because the temperature had reached 96 degrees that day, making the attic like an oven. Since there was no floor, I had to hop from stud to stud, stepping on an occasional board. To complicate matters, the space was dimly lit, with only a glimmer of twilight coming in a small stained glass window at each end of the attic. When I reached the large box, I saw that it contained many smaller boxes of quarters, dimes, and nickels. I made trip after trip carrying these heavy little boxes, trying to keep my balance as I picked my way across the studs and planks. A couple of times I almost slipped and put a foot through the ceiling into a bedroom below. After a dozen trips in the stifling heat, I was drenched with sweat. The whole episode began to assume a bizarre, dreamlike quality, as though I had been condemned to move coins forever about a dark Hades as penance for having been born a Krotter. I finally reached the bottom of the box, however, and we then stashed away all the coins out of sight of Dad and the girls. Hot, sweaty, and exhausted, I went down to the living room to join Dad and his guest, both of whom remained unaware of what had been happening overhead.

The next major problem was to convince Dad to come to New England with us to enter a nursing home. He kept insisting he wanted to stay in Palisade, but this was impossible since we could find no one to take care of him. In addition to being very frail and confused, he had a urinary catheter that needed constant attention, so nursing home care seemed best. Fortunately, Dad happened that week to read a book on the role of stress in heart attacks and decided he would be subject to less stress if he returned with us to enter a nursing home.

On our final day in Palisade, we tried to finish up as many jobs as possible. Around 4 o'clock in the afternoon, Wells and I made a final survey of the town house basement. We again saw the boxes of orange marmalade piled on the shelves in the back storage room and debated whether we should take the time to load them on the last dump truck we were filling. First Wells said, "Oh, it's so late, let's just have Clark Brown take them to the dump another day." Then we decided just to do it ourselves, so we started carrying out the boxes. To our great surprise and amusement, we discovered that the rear boxes contained not jars of orange marmalade, but bags of silver quarters. It seemed an appropriate ending to both the orange marmalade saga and the labors of the summer.

CHAPTER FOURTEEN

After that horrendous and exhausting month in Nebraska, we were relieved to be heading back to New England at the end of August of 1978. We took the train to Lincoln with Dad and then changed to an airplane for the rest of our trip. Dad had always been afraid to fly, so I watched his demeanor on takeoff with some concern. He was so engrossed in reading a book on inflation, however, he did not even glance out the window.

That evening we arrived at Dad's nursing home in Freeport, Maine. As we were walking down the hall to his room, the nurse asked him about the book he was carrying. He immediately proceeded to give her his lecture on inflation. She must have realized then that Dad was no ordinary nursing home patient.

Fortunately, the staff was very tolerant of Dad's habits, and before long his bureau contained stacks of *Forbes, Business Week*, and *Barron's*. He spent most of that year sitting in his room and studying his magazines and investment books. His mental attitude was remarkably positive. Instead of finding it depressing to share his dining room table with three rather pitiful women in various states of deterioration, he was as delighted as a child that he could eat up the rice pudding or jello they didn't want. On holidays and other occasions, he enjoyed spending time with us at our home. All year long he said to me, "I'm going to study and keep my mind active because I'm going home to Nebraska next summer." He did make great physical and mental progress that year, and by spring he was able to have the catheter removed.

I was glad I could supervise Dad's care in a nursing home near us that year to help take the burden off Diane. As usual she and I were the ones taking care of Mom and Dad because Kent with his alcoholic problems was no help and Mark never came down from Canada.

Things were happening in Mark's life that caused him to withdraw further from the family. During the sabbatical year that we spent in Cambridge, England, Mark and Margaret had left Vancouver to spend a year in New Zealand. Margaret had just graduated from medical school and wanted to spend a year in New Zealand as an intern. Mark arranged for a year's leave of absence from his job as a public prosecutor so that he could enter a master's-in-law program in New Zealand. We later heard that Margaret had been upset when Mark arrived in New Zealand and announced that he couldn't find an appropriate master's program in the city where she was interning and would instead be studying in another city and commuting to spend weekends with her. They had already been living apart for a couple of months because Margaret had had to leave for New Zealand before Mark was free to leave his job. This time spent apart probably contributed to the collapse of their marriage. When there was an ocean between Mark and Margaret, she apparently began to reflect more upon their life together. Part of the problem was that she had been only about nineteen when she met Mark while they were both spending the summer working in a lodge in the Canadian Rockies. I suspect that her dating experience had been limited because she once remarked to Diane that men who appreciated smart women were as "scarce as hen's teeth." At any rate, when she decided to marry Mark, she probably had had little opportunity to compare him to other potential husbands.

During the year that we were in Cambridge, England, Margaret's parents happened to be in London, where her father was working for a Canadian firm. One day that spring we invited them to come out to Cambridge for lunch. As we were eating, she remarked about what a shame it was that Mark and Margaret had separated. "What do you mean?" I exclaimed. Wells and I had been totally unaware that they were having problems. When Margaret's mother and I went for a walk that afternoon along the public footpath that crossed our orchard, I heard a few more details about what had happened.

Margaret's mother told me that Margaret had complained that Mark never wanted to go to parties or to do things with friends. He had always been a loner, and once he was married he was perfectly content just to do things with Margaret. She was more socially inclined, however, and was not happy with this arrangement. The parallels to my parents' marriage were painfully apparent. Even though neither Kent nor Mark had much feeling for their father, they shared many of his habits and personality and character traits. I even heard from Margaret's mother that Mark had had Margaret pack up all his hundreds of books to put them in storage before they left for New Zealand.

As soon as I learned of Mark's marital problems, I wrote to tell him how sorry I was because I knew what an ideal wife Margaret had seemed to be for him and how much he loved her. I also immediately called Diane, who despite my advice, had been threatening to write to tell Mark off for not offering more help or at least expressing more concern during Dad's present illness. Unfortunately, I was too late; she had sent the letter a couple of days earlier. It was the last thing Mark needed at that point. As was increasingly typical of Diane, she didn't even say she was sorry she had sent it, but instead asserted that it was better to get these things said. Mark later sent me a copy of the letter. In painfully emotional terms, Diane not only strongly criticized him for not loving his parents enough, but also indirectly expressed her fear that he didn't love her enough either. She ended by saying that tears were streaming down her face as she wrote.

Mark never responded to my letter offering sympathy for his marital problems. In fact, he never again mentioned Margaret and their relationship to me. For the first couple of months after I heard the news from his mother-in-law, I occasionally got further bits of information from her. She reported that Mark was confiding in her how devastated he was that Margaret wanted to end the marriage. Finally, when Margaret's mother realized that Mark wasn't telling his family anything about the situation, she understandably stopped offering me information about what was going on.

Mom was very sad to learn of Mark and Margaret's separation and eventual divorce, but I wonder if her grief on his behalf wasn't tinged with a peculiar realization that Margaret had boldly taken the step she herself had decided not to take some forty-five years earlier.

That summer when we had returned from Europe to Nebraska to find the gold and silver and handle all Dad's affairs, a Canadian attorney sent us a letter to inquire about some details of the estate business and to say that Mark would deal with us henceforth through him. My call to the lawyer confirmed that Mark wanted no further contact with the family and wished us to have neither his address nor phone number. There were moments when I even doubted if he were still alive and wondered if he had committed suicide, leaving an elaborate cover-up behind him. Every Christmas thereafter, his only gift to Mom and Dad was a subscription to the magazine *Beautiful British Columbia*. This seemed increasingly ironic, as the last thing he wanted was to have them visit him in Vancouver. He never wrote either of them, nor did he ever telephone them. Mom's life was greatly saddened by this, but in her gallant way, she continually defended Mark's behavior, saying there must be some reason for it. Given everything she had done for him over the years, his actions seemed incomprehensible to me. Dad also loved Mark very much and always showed his picture to everyone and talked about him. Fortunately, we succeeded in keeping Dad from ever learning of his divorce. Until he died, he was still talking about taking the train up to Canada to visit Mark.

I found it particularly puzzling that Mark was withdrawing from contact with me because the two of us had had a very close relationship when he was growing up. Since I was eight years older than he, I was often given the responsibility of taking care of him, and he frequently called me "Mom" by mistake.

After Mark severed ties with us, everyone in the family speculated endlessly about his seemingly inexplicable actions, our conversations revolving in the same unproductive circles. I think that over the ensuing years we would have felt better to have known the reasons for his conduct, no matter how much we might have disagreed with them. Instead we were left forever flitting from one theory to another, none of which ever seemed to make much sense. We knew how much he loved Margaret but saw no reason for him to turn his back on us because she had left him. I sometimes wondered if he in some way blamed his family or his upbringing for his loss of Margaret. Perhaps in a moment of anger, she had said something like "You're just like your father, and if I stay with you, I might end up like your mother!"

CHAPTER FIFTEEN

Back to Nebraska we headed with Dad in June of 1979. Wells and I planned to spend a week in Palisade cleaning out the remaining Main Street buildings and selling many of the excess books before taking Dad to Estes Park with us for the summer. The previous summer we had gathered up almost 6,000 books scattered throughout various buildings and had lined them up on the shelves of the old drugstore. This drugstore had been a very important place in my childhood. It was only a couple of doors down from Dad's office, and one of his partners would sometimes give me a nickel to go buy an ice cream cone. Then when I was a teenager I would often stop in the drugstore after school to have a soda with a friend. It now seemed very strange to have such a public place transformed into a private Krotter space.

We had decided to sell these 6,000 books we had gathered in the drugstore, but we planned to keep Dad's better ones, which were in the town house. That winter I had talked by phone with a used-book dealer from Denver named John Blythe. As he was planning to pass near Palisade on a trip with his partner, he agreed to stop and look at the books. After they had seen the books we were selling and the others remaining in the town house, Mr. Blythe called me to say how absolutely amazed they had been to find a library of that quality in a quiet little Nebraska town in the middle of nowhere. They were particularly astounded when they entered the small upstairs room where we had piled a couple hundred Limited Edition Club books still in their original red mailing wrappers. Mr. Blythe exclaimed, "No one in the book business will ever believe we were surrounded by that many Limited Edition Club books that had never been unwrapped!"

As it turned out, we sold Mr. Blythe not only the 6,000 books, but also one of our Main Street buildings. Coming from Denver, he could not believe the price of Palisade real estate. He really wanted to buy the drugstore building, with its ornamental pressed-tin ceiling, but we had already sold it, so we showed him the theater building. He considered it a real bargain at $7,000. The old brass and steel projector fascinated him; he said it was just the kind of curiosity a Denver bar would buy for decoration.

Our main cleaning job that summer was to clear out the lumberyard buildings so the yard could be sold. As with the drugstore, it gave me a very odd feeling to have Dad's lumberyard take on a completely different function in my life. When I was a child, my cousin Linda and I used to have great fun playing hide-and-seek among the piles of lumber. As I grew up, I realized the lumberyard's importance as the head office for all Dad's business interests in southwest Nebraska. He spent most of his time in his back office, keeping the books for his company. Now the lumberyard was just one more piece of property that had to be cleaned out and dealt with.

On one side of the lumberyard was a large two-story brick building with lumber stock stored on the first floor. The upper floor had originally been rented out as a lodge hall, but for the past twenty years, Dad had just used it for storage. It was only half-full of newspapers and magazines; even Dad could not subscribe to enough publications to fill all his Main Street buildings. By this point we were really tired of carrying heavy loads up and down stairs, so we drove the dump truck into the lumberyard and backed it up under an upstairs window. Then we could throw armfuls of newspapers and magazines out the window onto the truck below. It was even fun for the first half-hour. Passersby on Main Street watched curiously as the newspapers and magazines came cascading out of the window onto the truck below. Our annual summer appearance was becoming an eagerly awaited break in the monotony of life in Palisade.

In addition to the books and newspapers, Dad had also stored in this building a couple dozen boxes, many of them still unopened, containing pictures and sculptures he had ordered from the Collector's Club. Through its slick catalogues, this company attempts to convince people they are purchasing art objects that will be a good investment. Dad had put a few thousand dollars into their offerings, and we were lucky to sell what he had bought at 40 percent of his purchase price. It was sickening to look at all the invoices for $80 or $100 on boxes that had never been opened, but just stuck away in a dusty corner to be forgotten for years. Once again we were struck by this sheer waste in a world where so many people were struggling to get enough to eat. Even my mother had always spent money very carefully for someone in her position, denying herself many things she would have liked to buy. One spring I wanted her to come to Maine to see us, but she said Dad didn't want her to spend the money at that point. Two or three of these unopened pictures would have paid for her ticket.

We had always been frustrated to see Dad throw money away on many occasions and be inexplicably tightfisted at other times. During the first eight years my grandparents Musick lived in the little house behind us, there was a bathroom only in the basement. Since my grandmother was unable to climb stairs, she had to use a chamber pot all those years. Mom begged Dad to have a bathroom installed in the corner of the bedroom, but he did so only after my grandmother had a stroke.

After Wells and I moved all the Collectors Club boxes back over to the main house, we turned our attention to the basement of the lumber-yard office. It was actually a very large double basement that also extended under the post office. Thinking we were less likely to find coins here, we hired three teenagers to help carry loads up the stairs and throw them onto the dump truck. The logistics of this job were parti-cularly difficult because the main part of the basement lay beyond a sunken area eighteen inches deep that contained the coal furnace. To get across this pit, we had to walk on a plank while bending down to avoid hitting our heads on the heating ducts above. It was exhausting work to carry a heavy box across this plank while bending over, then climb the basement stairs with the load, and finally heave it up onto the truck. To make matters worse, everything in the basement was covered with a thick layer of coal dust that had been gathering for decades. Within a few minutes, we all looked like chimney sweeps, with sooty smudges all over our faces and arms and black coal dust sprinkled on our hair and eyebrows.

The contents of that basement were a strange conglomeration. We found everything from old globe street lights to mixing bowls still in their original boxes. Much of the accumulation was manufacturers' samples of objects like shingles or storm windows. There were gallons and gallons of old paint. For half a century, people had been putting unwanted items down there and forgetting about them; the basement had probably never before been cleaned. Dozens of boxes of musty business records contained invoices as much as forty years old.

To complicate our efforts, we had to work around Dad, who was sufficiently improved mentally to be more aware of our activities that summer. He didn't approve of our throwing anything away, of course, but there wasn't much he could do about it. We had him outnumbered. As always, Dad thought everything would have an eventual use if one saved it long enough, so he kept trying to rescue things as we carried the loads by him. When Dad saw that we had thrown away a stack of ring binders containing old sales information, he wanted to throw away the papers and save the binders. Finally, he found a pitchfork and worked patiently to spear the rings of the notebooks and drag them off the truck. We couldn't help feeling sorry for him, but we were exasperated to have him slowing down the whole operation. By midmorning we were so hot and exhausted that we found it particularly annoying to have him inspecting every load we threw on. Pretty soon he went over to the house and got a butcher knife to open boxes. Before long, he was standing by the back of the truck, waving his butcher knife as he gesticulated his unhappiness with each successive load heaved onto the truck. I knew he wasn't meaning to threaten anyone with the knife, but I thought it might intimidate our young workers, so when he went to the bathroom I hid it behind a pile of bricks.

As it turned out, Dad's time was well spent that day. While we were throwing out junk, he found a safe he had filled with valuables a few years earlier. It was in a small storeroom at the foot of the basement stairs, a room full of business records. Like most of Dad's other caches, the safe was concealed by piles of junk that protected it from thieves. This safe was not even locked, even though it contained $20,000 worth of gold coins and a couple of very large diamonds. Our teenage helpers would have been amazed if they had known that a few feet from their well-trodden path lay a small fortune.

Since we didn't want to take the time to clear out the hardware basement and thought it a less likely hiding place for coins, we asked my cousin Fred to get some men from the ranch to cart everything away after our departure. Fred later reported that they had cleared almost everything away when they came to a box in a corner that appeared to contain business records. Fred decided to carry it over to the lumberyard office, but found it too heavy to pick up. Lifting up the top layer of business papers, he discovered coins concealed below. It was about five o'clock in the afternoon, so he went across to the bank to see if the owners were still there. Finding they had not yet left, he got a garbage can and put the coins in it. While Fred and one of his helpers were carrying this awkward load across the middle of Main Street, one of them stepped on the other's toe, and in the confusion, the garbage can overturned, spilling coins in all directions. Luckily, Main Street happened to be deserted at that hour, so Fred didn't have to come up with an explanation for his garbage can full of coins.

There was one other building we wanted to check carefully ourselves; this was the large double garage next to the house. One side had always been kept locked, and Dad would never let anyone inside, so it seemed a likely place for valuables to be hidden. As we suspected, in a large packing crate just inside the door we found forty thousand silver nickels packed in ten-pound boxes.

As the end of our week in Palisade approached, we had to decide what to do with the valuables we had found. The boxes of nickels in the garage were far too heavy for us to take with us to Colorado, so we left them there temporarily. As that part of the garage had no windows and only the one front entrance right on the street, we thought it would be somewhat protected from burglary. We accepted Clark and Helen Brown's offer to have their daughter Shirley and her husband Jerry move the nickels to the local bank when they visited Palisade in a few weeks.

The gold coins and diamonds in the basement safe in the lumberyard office were a more pressing problem. Since he had rediscovered the safe, Dad had been proudly carrying around the diamonds, showing them to various neighbors. Wells and I decided it was safest to take the gold coins and diamonds to Colorado with us to add them to the rest of the collection in the bank vaults in Denver.

CHAPTER SIXTEEN

That Saturday we finished loading our last dump truck, number twenty-seven for the two summers. As we watched it head for the dump, we were immensely relieved to think that all the sorting and carrying it represented were behind us forever. Now we were free to leave the next morning to spend our summer vacation in Estes Park. Dad insisted he was going to stay in Palisade, but we didn't pay much attention because we had explained to him that we had not been able to find anyone who would take care of him there.

Early the next morning Dad made a trip over to the office. I assumed he was putting back the diamonds because they were no longer on top of his dresser. After Dad came back, Wells went over to get both the gold coins and the diamonds so that we could take them with us to Colorado. In ten minutes he returned with the gold coins, but said he couldn't find the diamonds. Sure that they must be there somewhere, I went over to see for myself, but I couldn't find them either. Back at the house, I looked more carefully in Dad's room and found the diamonds in the top drawer of his bureau, so I located Dad and suggested he take them back over to the safe. He duly shuffled over to the office to put them away. A few minutes after he returned, I made one more trip to the office basement and put the diamonds in my purse to take them to the bank in Colorado. It seemed like a bizarre game of "diamond, diamond, who's got the diamond?"

By eleven o'clock, I had the beds made, the dishes done, and the children dressed and ready to leave for Estes Park. Dad had other ideas, however. When we were all ready to go, he simply refused to budge, and for an hour we sat arguing with him. When noon came, we decided that we might as well all go over to the cafe to get something to eat since I had left no food in the house. When we went back home, Dad was still adamant that he was going to stay in Palisade. Wells and I were getting really frustrated and angry because we wanted to start the long drive to Colorado with the children before it got any later. It was much easier to open up the cabin during daylight, and Mom was expecting us to pick her up at her apartment in Estes Park late that afternoon before we went on out to the cabin. We were in a real bind because we couldn't get Dad to come and we couldn't go off and leave him.

After another half hour had passed, I maneuvered Dad out onto the front porch and then locked the door behind us all. This ruse didn't work; he just sat down in his porch chair and insisted he was going to stay right there. He said he could eat his meals at the restaurant and use their bathroom. In desperation I walked over to the home of the local banker, who was an old business friend of Dad's, to ask him to talk to Dad. I also knew he was in charge of the ambulance, and I had that in mind as a last resort. He came over to the house with me and sat down on the porch to talk to Dad, but was no more successful than we had been. Finally he gave up, saying, "Dean, if I weren't a church-going person, I'd say you were one hell of a stubborn man." As he left, he whispered to me that he would call some of the ambulance volunteers to help us because he agreed it was impossible for Dad to stay there by himself.

By this time, Dad was getting suspicious and headed off down the block. Leaving Wells to wait for the ambulance, I started after Dad, trailing him for a few blocks until he entered a friend's house. After a while, I saw the ambulance approaching and just then Dad came out of the house and saw it too. Even though his normal gait was a shuffle, he attempted to run down the street. Annoyed as I was with Dad, I felt terribly sorry for him as he tried so desperately to escape. He was no match for the ambulance attendants in their blue coats, however. They caught up with him immediately and loaded him kicking and flailing into the back seat of our car, which Wells had driven along behind. I had thought that the ambulance would take Dad at least part way to Colorado, but they decided just to follow us to the next town and leave us there if he had calmed down. After driving a few miles, we could see that Dad was going to give up and go quietly, so we signaled the ambulance to return to Palisade. Dad was so furious with us that he said he was going to starve himself. By the time we stopped at McDonald's three hours later, however, he was the first one out of the car.

This trying incident was only a prelude to another Colorado vacation filled with problems. By this point, Diane, Wells, and I were very weary of the endless sequence of family crises that had arisen one after the other with a harrowing similarity over the past nine years. But there was no avoiding the problems, and our chief one now was to find another living arrangement for Mom. Since her initial breakdown in 1970, she had lived in at least ten different places. Given her age and variable condition, it seemed advisable to find a more permanent situation. After some investigation, I discovered a good retirement facility called Fairview Terrace in northern Denver. We all felt relieved when Mom agreed she would move there in September.

That decision seemed easy compared to the far more troublesome problem of where Dad was going to live because he kept vociferously insisting he would live nowhere but in Palisade. The question about what legal control we had over him now arose. I had always assumed that Diane had obtained not just a conservatorship over his property, but also a guardianship over his person since he had brain damage. Now to my surprise I learned from Diane's lawyer, Raymond Hanson, that she did not in fact have control over his person. This meant that our ambulance operation getting Dad out of Palisade had not even been legal, but in a small town you can kidnap your own father without anyone asking a lot of questions.

Diane and I went down to Denver to discuss with Mr. Hanson the possibility of getting a guardianship over Dad. He discouraged us from such an attempt, saying it would require a long and costly legal battle that might not be successful. Diane then launched into a long tirade about how sick and tired she was of Dad making life difficult for everyone. She vehemently announced, "If he goes back to Palisade, I won't so much as send him a toothbrush." I finally said that Wells and I would go out to Palisade and make an all-out effort to locate someone to take care of Dad if he returned to his house. In addition, I volunteered to oversee all the details of his life in Palisade if we were successful. Diane agreed to that arrangement, which we implemented a couple of weeks later. We set up a secondary bank account for me to use for Dad's living expenses, and Diane funded this account from the conservatorship account.

A few days later Wells and I drove out to Palisade with the girls and started looking for someone to take care of Dad. Just as we were beginning to think that we would never find anyone, someone suggested Bonnie Ferguson, a middle-aged woman who had been recently widowed. We were delighted when she agreed to take the job. She proved to be kind, capable, and totally dependable during the four years she cared for Dad. Every morning and evening she went over to give him his medication and wash the dishes, and she also cleaned the house every week and did his laundry. He ate one meal a day at the restaurant and heated soup or something for his other meal. This arrangement worked out so well that I ended up respecting Dad's tenacity in fighting for the right to live in his own house. Of course, when we visited him during the next few summers, we were concerned to see charred spots on the floor near the fireplace where exploding embers had landed. It still seemed worth the risk to have him happily ensconced for the last four years of his life in the house in which he had been born.

CHAPTER SEVENTEEN

The gold and silver were still stacked in six very large vaults in the safe deposit area of our Denver bank. (Each vault had a capacity of at least twenty cubic feet.) We had occasionally considered having the collection appraised but had not done so, primarily because Diane didn't want any local coin dealers to know about the collection. By now she was as much of a gold-bug as Dad. Like him, she seemed to derive an emotional satisfaction from actually touching the gold and silver coins. In the fall of 1979, she announced to me that she intended to hand count the hoard to get a more accurate idea of what we owned.

The idea was clearly absurd. I said at once that I didn't think it was practical to sort and count two tons of coins by hand. It seemed about as efficient as trying to scrub a gym floor with a toothbrush. Diane was not to be deterred, however. Over the next few months, she spent untold hours in the vault area of the bank basement counting piles of coins. I was amazed when I saw how she had done it. Instead of counting up uniform amounts of like coins into bank bags, she simply counted the coins and put them back in the random containers in which she had found them. She would count the coins in a coffee can and then put 226 quarters back into the bottom of the can with a piece of paper on top saying "226 quarters." Next would come a layer of dimes with a piece of paper covering them saying "139 dimes." Then there might be a layer of nickels on top of the dimes. The next person who came along couldn't get the various denominations of coins out of the can without them all mixing together. She even left coins in boxes that were falling apart.

Later Diane told me she had thought that if she left the coins in their original containers, we might have more information about their source and quality. She even left a few dimes in the Smith Brothers cough box in which Dad had placed them. But we had hurriedly gathered up most of the coins in helter-skelter fashion, simply dumping them randomly into whatever containers were at hand. The whole hand-counting operation was all too typical of Diane's totally impractical nature. Even though she was afraid to have the bank handle the project because of her obsession with secrecy, we could have rented a machine to count and sort the coins accurately and efficiently.

Diane toiled away in the basement vaults for eight long months. Her telephone reports made it clear that she was feeling more and more like the little red hen as she spent endless hours shaking the dirt from the coins and carefully counting them. At last, she compiled a seventy- page inventory list stating how many coins each box or coffee can or milk carton contained. Although the inventory was useful, far too great an effort had been expended to produce it, and the coins were still not in marketable form.

When Diane sent me a list, I asked if she was going to file it with the probate court. She replied that she didn't think it advisable to provide the government with so much information. As always, she was operating from the same ultraconservative political viewpoint that Dad held. They both believed that if government officials found out you had gold and silver, they would some day confiscate it. As it was, the only information the probate court had about the collection was that there was $68,000 face value in gold and silver coins; this was only an early rough estimate based on counting the contents of one of six vaults. Now that more precise information was available, I thought Diane had a responsibility to give a more accurate figure to the court.

Diane also sent a copy of the inventory to Kent, a move that ulti- mately had the disastrous consequence of reducing the value of the hoard by at least $140,000. First, Kent immediately showed his copy to a con-man, who undoubtedly could hardly believe his good fortune. From that time on, he hardly let Kent out of his sight. Kent also showed the inventory to a coin dealer acquaintance named Jack Harrington. It seems likely that Kent was bolstering his low self-image by making people think he was going to inherit a large sum of money. At any rate, Jack Harrington was extremely interested. Kent soon called us with a proposal that he bring Jack out to Denver that summer to sort and appraise the coins. In addition, Jack had suggested that it would be smart to convert the hoard into rare coins because he maintained that the profit potential was greater there. Obviously, the profit potential was great for Jack because the conversion would have assured him a large commission.

There were many things wrong with this proposal. First of all, we would be taking coins we knew were genuine and exchanging them for coins whose authenticity might be questionable. I didn't think we should put ourselves in the position where we had to trust the word of someone we barely knew about the value of the rare coins he would procure for us. Investing in rare coins is no field for the novice, and the mere fact that the rare coin market had done well recently did not mean that it would continue to do so. The other obvious objection was that we would have to pay a large tax on the conversion.

I was dubious about Kent's judgment and thought he might be overly trusting of his coin dealer friend. Every time Kent called he mentioned some new proposal Jack had made concerning our collection. Kent thought Jack was very clever; I thought he was probably just a fast talker.

Kent seemed unusually excited about the whole issue. Every day or two he called to try to persuade us to let Jack and him handle the collection, urging us to decide quickly so that Jack could come to Colorado before he attended the summer coin shows. He suggested that the two of them could stay at Diane's house and take home gold coins to grade every evening. This plan to remove coins from the vaults was particularly alarming since we knew nothing about Jack Harrington's integrity. I told Diane's lawyer, Raymond Hanson, that if the plan went forward without further investigation, I would complain to the probate judge. I thought that we needed to have an expert look at the collection, but to have Kent, of all people, choose our expert seemed foolish and dangerous. Of course, it would have been logical to choose a Denver coin dealer, someone with a respected reputation in the community. Unfortunately, Diane as usual resisted the idea of dealing with anyone in Denver because she didn't want anyone local to know about the collection. From the beginning, her desire for total privacy led to disastrous decisions.

When I insisted we not rush into this arrangement with Jack, the plan was dropped. A year later I learned that during these negotiations Diane had suddenly found out Kent was drinking again. This undoubtedly gave her another reason not to proceed. Once again she had failed to share crucial information about Kent's drinking with me. At any rate, Kent was extremely upset when the plan was dropped. I think he had an intense urge to get involved with the coins, to actually hold them in his hands, a desire arising from his deep-seated psychological entanglement with gold and silver.

*   *   *   *

That summer I invited Dad to spend a week with us in Estes Park. Wells and I could hardly keep from laughing aloud when he announced his new project. He was collecting copper pennies because the copper content was worth more than a penny and might soon increase even further in value. Here we go again, we thought. Another financial plan also had him excited. In his office he had found two old $20 gold certificates dating from the 1920s. (They resemble an ordinary $20 bill except that the words "redeemable in gold" are printed on them.) The government had just started selling one-ounce gold medallions in post offices, so Dad thought he should be able to turn in each of his $20 gold certificates to the post office for a gold medallion worth about $500. He reasoned thus: at the time the gold certificates were issued, they could be redeemed for a $20 gold piece, containing one ounce of gold, so why shouldn't the government now give him a one-ounce gold medallion for each?

Dad was much stronger now; living in his own home had clearly been beneficial to him. His housekeeper Bonnie Ferguson reported to me that he frequently walked a three-mile circuit. This summer I was having trouble keeping him from overexerting in the high altitude. His doctor had assured me that he could come to the mountains as long as he didn't try to climb uphill. The first morning, however, Dad got up at dawn before everyone else, walked down our road to throw off rocks, and then walked back uphill to get home. One morning he suddenly announced he was going to walk to town, four and a half miles away, to buy his favorite business magazine, *Barron's*, and prune juice. I was so busy trying to keep him from leaving that I didn't realize what an amusing combination of purchases it was until Wells later pointed it out. He often saw the humor of a situation before the rest of us since he could remain more detached from our family problems. The first summer we were working in Palisade, the upstairs toilet wouldn't flush. We had to pour buckets of water down it for a couple of weeks until a plumber from McCook could come to fix it. "Here you have all this gold and silver," laughed Wells, "and the toilet doesn't even flush."

One day Dad slipped away from us after breakfast. When he didn't return, we began to look around but saw no sign of him. We drove toward town, looking all along the road with no result. I asked about him at a grocery store on the edge of town, thinking he might have gone in after prune juice, but they had not seen him. We started driving back home, stopping to inquire at a couple of stores and filling stations. Just as the cashier in one store was saying she hadn't seen Dad, a customer spoke up and said she thought she had seen him an hour or so ago. While eating a late breakfast in a roadside restaurant, she had noticed an elderly man shuffling along the road to town, looking hot and tired. That had to be Dad, so we turned back toward town. Before long we saw him walking along on his way home. When I asked him what in the world he was doing, he explained that he had walked downtown to the post office to see if they would give him two gold medallions in exchange for his gold certificates. The postal employees had told him they didn't know anything about gold certificates and had suggested he inquire in Denver at either the main post office or the Federal Reserve branch bank.

Dad was now determined to go to Denver to trade in his certificates for gold. I had no choice but to go with him because I didn't want him wandering the streets alone on a fool's errand.

As soon as we arrived in Denver, Dad headed to the main post office. He explained his errand to a clerk at a window, who then led him into an office to talk to a higher authority. Since I did not want to be drawn into the gold certificate controversy, I remained in the lobby. Not knowing what to make of the gold certificates, the officials finally suggested Dad inquire at the Federal Reserve branch bank, so off we went on yet another wild goose chase.

I had no idea what a Federal Reserve branch bank looked like and was surprised to find a hushed atmosphere more suggestive of a temple than a bank. There were no long lines of customers waiting for tellers to handle their transactions. The minute we entered the door, an armed guard approached us and asked our business. After Dad explained his mission, the guard informed him that he would have to talk to an officer in charge of monetary policy, who was located on the second floor. Since the general public was not allowed access to that floor, Dad had to communicate with the officer by telephone. He was unhappy about that arrangement but had no other choice. After listening to Dad's complicated exchange plan, the officer told him that the government had stopped honoring the gold redemption clause on gold certificates when the country went off the gold standard in 1932. Dad attempted to argue the ethics of the matter but eventually had to give up. The man on the other end of the phone clearly had no intention of giving him any gold.

CHAPTER EIGHTEEN

The year 1980 was an eventful one in the metals market. In early January, gold and silver prices began to skyrocket. Gold ultimately reached $850 an ounce, and silver hit $48 an ounce when the Hunt brothers of Texas cornered the market. As the markets went up, I spent hours calculating the advantages of selling part of our collection. As always, the problem with selling was that we would have to pay almost 20 percent of the sales price in capital gains tax, whereas this tax would never be paid if we held the metals until Dad's death. The way these prices were jumping, however, our tax bill would be no more than the amount the metals had risen in two or three days.

During the week of the meteoric price increases, I was on the phone every day with Diane. I tried to convince her to sell part of the collection, but she was reluctant to do so. To gold-bugs no time ever seems to be propitious for selling. Low prices offer an excellent buying opportunity, while rapidly rising prices confirm all their fears that the economy is about to collapse and the banks to fail, propelling gold to $2000 an ounce or some other stratospheric level.

Through the intermediary of Franz Pick, a leading monetary expert who had known Dad over the years, I contacted a dealer at the prestigious firm of Mocatta Metals. He offered me twenty-four times face value on our 90-percent silver coins and comparable prices on our silver nickels and gold. After our conversation, I made some calculations based on Diane's inventory sheets and discovered that if we were to sell all the collection at these prices, we would receive about $1,000,000 for the silver and $500,000 for the gold.

Prices like these were an exciting prospect; I was convinced that we should quickly sell at least half the collection. Unfortunately, only Wells and I could see the necessity to act at once in this volatile market. Whenever I talked to Diane, she said that she didn't want to act hastily. She asked me to talk to Raymond Hanson, her conservatorship lawyer, but my conversations with him were equally frustrating. He pondered about whether Diane should go to the probate judge for permission to sell. Since a conservator has the power to carry out normal business, this seemed unnecessary, but it could have been done quickly if he thought it essential. Raymond also suggested getting the collection appraised before any large amounts were sold, but we couldn't afford to take that much time in this volatile market. We were reasonably sure that the bulk of Dad's hoard was "junk" silver, and we couldn't go far wrong selling this portion without an appraisal. And it wouldn't have required more than a few hours for Diane to take a selected sample of gold and silver coins to a couple of Denver dealers to obtain an opinion about the general quality of our coins. I was highly impatient with Raymond's dilatory attitude and insisted that if he thought the judge should be consulted, they should do so posthaste because the market would not go up forever.

By the weekend of January 25, I was still pushing Diane to sell a substantial portion of the collection. At last I was beginning to make a little progress, but the whole process had just been too slow. That Monday morning the metals market fell sharply and the wisdom of selling became more debatable. On January 15 and 22, Wells and I had sold out our entire portfolio of 600 shares of stock in the Homestake Mining Company, the principal U.S. gold mining company. It was enormously frustrating to us then and over the ensuing years to think we had played the market correctly with the only gold and silver interests we controlled but had been powerless to sell my father's precious metals when their value peaked above $1,500,000. And to compound our regrets, interest rates were at an all-time high at that point, so we missed the chance to put our proceeds into Treasury Bills at 14 percent interest and be financially secure for life.

Since Raymond kept insisting that we needed to obtain a higher statement of value for the collection to give to the judge before selling anything, I immediately moved in this direction. It would have been quickest and easiest just to use a Denver appraiser, but Diane was still paranoid about local involvement. After some thought, I suggested we consider Stack's coin store in New York, where Dad had purchased almost all his gold coins. Since the firm was one of the oldest and most prestigious in the country, it seemed a logical choice.

When Diane agreed that I could make preliminary inquiries, I called Charles Stack. He immediately said, "Oh, I remember your father very well." No one ever forgot Dad. Mr. Stack agreed to spend a day or two at the beginning of March looking over the hoard, as he insisted on calling it. He did not make a detailed appraisal, but after viewing the coins and looking at Diane's inventory sheets, he gave us a letter indicating a current value of $750,000-$800,000, with a possibility that it might be as high as $1,000,000 on closer inspection. The value of the collection had dropped precipitously from its peak in January because gold had by now fallen from $850 an ounce to $600 an ounce and silver had declined from $48 an ounce to $18 an ounce. Our silver coins that had been worth a million dollars a few weeks before had now dropped to a value of $350,000, so we had lost a small fortune by Diane's failure to act.

Mr. Stack thought the junk silver needed to be counted and bagged so that it would be in a marketable form. He proposed sending out a couple of men from New York to do this, but as that would be very expensive, Wells and I said we would be willing to handle the project.

Thus in late June of 1980 we spent two days at the bank, reorganizing the collection. We rented a machine to sort and count the coins, which Wells ran almost continuously for eight hours each day, pushing through the quarters, dimes, and nickels while I unwrapped boxes of coins and broke open hundreds of coin rolls. I went endlessly back and forth carrying containers of coins from the vault room where Diane was guarding the open vaults to the large room where Wells was running the coin counter, which rumbled and clanked away like some great metal animal swallowing coins as fast as we could supply them. Meanwhile, the vault employees looked on in curious disbelief.

When lunchtime arrived, an argument broke out over a trivial issue. Diane wanted to go out for lunch, but Wells wished to run the machine continuously. It was tedious work shoveling piles of coins covered with Nebraska dirt into a noisy machine in the hot and stuffy bank basement. Having reluctantly agreed to use some of his vacation time to sort the coins, Wells wanted to work as steadily as possible. If I went out and got sandwiches for all of us, he could keep the expensive machine running. He was right to feel the time pressure since we didn't quite finish sorting all the collection in the allotted two days. Unfortunately, Diane couldn't just go off to lunch by herself, leaving us to work, because she was the only one with legal access to the vaults at that point.

After conferring with Wells, I went back to the vaults to tell Diane that we wanted to keep working through lunch, eating sandwiches there.

She finally conceded, but she was livid, and the depth of her anger over the question of a chicken sandwich perplexed me. As on prior occasions, she furiously asserted, "This is absolutely the last time I'm doing anything for this family. This is it!"

During those two days, it became increasingly apparent that Diane deeply resented our whole sorting operation. She had worn herself out for eight months spending untold hours hand-counting the hoard. Then Wells and I rented a machine and carried out the whole operation in two days, ending up with the coins neatly bagged in uniform amounts, instead of all mixed together in coffee cans and cigar boxes and milk cartons.

Over the years Diane's relationship with me had changed. Although we had had a very close relationship as children, by my mid-teen years an unfortunate pattern had developed. Since Diane was never a practical person, Mom and I managed practical affairs for her. We had to chauffeur her around wherever she wanted to go. When Diane moved into a new apartment, it was Mom who got the place organized. After four years of postgraduate study in music and creative writing spent in six different places, Diane did not have a job or a practical plan for getting one, although she thought she would like to teach piano on the college level. Being concerned that she was drifting aimlessly from one course of study to another, I typed up letters of inquiry for her, had her sign them, and sent them off to various schools. One of these letters did land her a job in Denver, where she ultimately settled into private piano teaching.

Of course, in this kind of a relationship the dependent person sooner or later begins to resent the people who are taking charge, just as the practical person resents always having to take care of someone else. Even when I told myself I was going to let Diane do just as she pleased, situations would arise when I would have to bite my tongue to keep from offering a suggestion. She went around the city streets carrying a purse stuffed so full she couldn't close it, a walking invitation to a pickpocket. It especially made me nervous when the open purse contained the keys to the vaults containing a fortune in gold and silver.

One of the underlying problems in our relationship was that Diane was not a happy person and was frequently depressed, so it was difficult for her to relate well to others. She was an excellent piano teacher, but this was not what she had wanted to do with her life. When she was growing up, my parents and grandparents had always talked about her becoming a concert pianist because she was very talented. Of course, in that area of rural Nebraska, she seemed like a prodigy, but the family view of her as a future concert pianist was hardly realistic. She did study piano with a leading New York teacher for a year after graduating from college, but she soon realized that she had no chance of making it to the top as a pianist. She had always been interested in writing and had won a couple of prizes in college, so as she got older her goal changed to becoming a writer. She started spending most of her free time writing and eventually wrote two novels. She was unable to get them published, however, and found this enormously frustrating.

I sometimes wondered if Diane were not envious that I had made a good marriage and had children. She had always disclaimed any interest in marriage, and Mom often remarked that Diane would resent having to put aside her writing to change a diaper or prepare a meal. On the other hand, she had a strong, unsatisfied need for affection, and I think she realized I had something wonderful in my relationships with my husband and children that she would never have. At any rate, as soon as I was married, she began to distance herself from me.

All these elements of our relationship were involved when we began managing Dad's estate. She held the actual power as conservatrix, but I managed most of the practical details, such as organizing the sale of the lumberyards. When Diane exploded the day we were sorting coins, it was probably because I had once again taken charge of a situation she was unable to handle effectively.

By the end of the second day, we had bagged all the loose quarters, dimes, and nickels. We had planned to empty one or two of the six large vaults, but we ran short of time when the bank officials insisted we close our vaults so that they could start their ritual of shutting the huge brass doors of the safe deposit area. We hastily threw some empty bags and a few coins back into the one vault we had already cleared and had no time to consolidate things to clear another.

As we were leaving the bank, I suggested to Diane that I could come back to Denver in a few days so we could rearrange things and empty a couple of vaults. She replied angrily, "I spent a tremendous amount of time and effort organizing the collection, and now Wells and you come in and move everything around. I'm just not going to have anything more to do with it." Thus we wasted $700 renting two very large vaults needlessly for the next couple of years. The following summer I again suggested we consolidate the vaults, but I met the same stubborn resistance.

It would hardly have been fair had we spent all our time handling Dad's gold and silver while neglecting him personally. Wells and I invited him to come out to Estes Park that summer as usual to spend a week with us and the girls. Dad also loved to have us visit him in Palisade, so that summer we again planned a trip home. All year long he saved up things to show us. During each visit, he regaled us with objects from his china closet. One by one he brought out the hand-painted floral plates that had belonged to his mother and the Wedgewood vases and Meissen figurines his aunt had bought during her frequent travels in Europe. Before long the dining room table would be piled high with china. Then he would bring out his favorite Limited Edition Club books for us to admire, as well as all his latest business and economic books. He hadn't changed in that respect; he still barely let you get in the door before he put a book in your hand.

Dad's eccentric purchasing tendencies were not lessening with age. In his kitchen cupboards, I counted fifty-six boxes of cereal, ten of one brand alone. (He could get a free plastic bowl for ten of those box tops.) His housekeeper continually threw out wormy boxes of cereal. The cupboard shelves held twenty-six jars of wheat germ, priced at $1.30 each. Although he drank only one cup of coffee a day, there were five three-pound cans of coffee sitting on the shelf. When I opened the pantry cupboards, a strong rancid odor emanated from a half-dozen one-pound bags of potato chips. Dad still couldn't resist buying in quantity when something was on sale.

Dad had fallen into another eccentric habit. He was putting his coffee grounds, orange rinds, and egg shells around the base of the black walnut tree on the front lawn for fertilizer. Unfortunately, the tree was located only a few feet from the main sidewalk to Main Street, so the townspeople had to look at all this decaying garbage surrounded by weed-choked buffalo grass as they came and went. I told Dad he couldn't put garbage on the front lawn, but I know he did as he pleased once I left town.

CHAPTER NINETEEN

Our search for gold and silver was several years behind us, but I was still having recurring nightmares about it. When I was younger, I often dreamed I was digging in the earth and unexpectedly found coins. Now I dreamed I was cleaning out one of the Palisade houses when I suddenly discovered a secret room piled high with things to be sorted. Occasionally, I would stumble upon a whole mysterious wing of the town house that I had never before seen. Once I dreamed I was wandering around the basement of the town house and discovered a dusty labyrinth of crumbling tunnels. There was always the haunting question whether there was gold and silver hidden in these secret places.

Money and family problems remained linked not only in my dreams, but also in reality. Kent made a strange phone call to me in the spring of 1981, asking for a loan. He offered to pay me one percent above the going Treasury Bill rate of interest, and as security he proposed his share of the Estes Park property, which I had often offered to buy. Although he wouldn't tell me just what he wanted the money for, he implied he wanted to get in on some hot business deal right away. He mentioned the sum of $25,000 but said he would take however much I could loan him. Although there was some chance of acquiring his share of Estes this way, Wells and I decided the whole idea was highly dubious and told Kent we weren't interested.

That April, Mom decided once again to stop taking her prescribed lithium and had to be hospitalized as a result. The evening she was admitted she called me collect from the hospital. "Alison, Alison," she gasped, "I can't breathe in this room. There isn't any oxygen. You've got to get me out of here, or I'll be dead by morning." Nothing I could say had any effect upon her wild mood. Diane and I always tried to persuade Mom that she couldn't go off lithium without disastrous consequences, but she remembered so little about her bad states that she had no realization of the enormous problems she caused us when she stopped her medication. Short of saying, "You're going to be stark, raving mad if you don't take lithium, Mom," there seemed to be no way we could make a strong enough impression upon her.

As the summer of 1981 approached, Diane announced that she no longer wanted to share the cabin with us but preferred instead to divide the summer in half. Mom and Dad had given the cabin to us four children several years earlier, but Diane and I were the only ones who used it. The main house contained four bedrooms, sleeping eight people, and two bathrooms. In addition, we had two outside guest cabins, each containing bathrooms. There was plenty of room for everyone to share the property, but Diane was adamant that she was spending no time with us.

One incident that summer indicates the friction now intensifying between us. Mom and I had spent a night at Diane's house in Denver. The next morning at breakfast I asked Diane for a check to replenish the account I kept to pay Dad's expenses. A half-hour later, as nine o'clock was approaching, I realized that she probably had a piano student arriving in a few minutes. I had to have the check before she started teaching because I was going to be leaving shortly thereafter and could not pay Dad's housekeeper on time without the money. So I said, "Don't forget to write me out that check before you start teaching, Diane." At that she exploded, saying in biting tones, "If you mention that check once more, you can take it and shove it up your you-know-what!" The fury of her outburst astonished not only me but also Mom, who later agreed I had done nothing to provoke the violence of Diane's response.

This kind of reaction made me wonder if I even wanted to live in the same cabin with Diane. It turned out that she left me no choice, adamantly insisting she would not share with us. We finally decided to build both a kitchen and bunkroom onto the small upper guest cabin so that the five of us could use it during the month of August, leaving Diane in possession of the main cabin.

While we were busy building this addition to the guest cabin early that July, problems again arose with Kent. He called to say he was in desperate straits and asked me to send him some money from Mom since I managed most of her funds in a power-of-attorney account. I knew that she usually responded to this kind of appeal from Kent and that she planned to make an annual exclusion gift of $3,000 to each of us soon. Hence I sent Kent a check for $3,000. Since Mom's mental condition was not good, I didn't mention the episode to her until she was again well. Before long, however, Kent was on the phone again, needing more money. This time he mentioned that he had offered to sell his share of Estes Park to Diane but she had not seemed inclined to buy it. This was surprising news. When I had talked to her a few days earlier about his request for the $3,000, she had divulged neither the fact that he had offered to sell her his share of Estes Park nor her knowledge that he was again drinking.

I reminded Kent that I had always been interested in buying his share of Estes Park and would still like to, if we could agree on a price. The question then arose whether Wells and I should purchase his share by ourselves or jointly with Diane. Since Mark remained an unknown quantity and did not communicate with us, he was out of the picture. We had enough money to buy Kent's entire share, but it seemed likely Diane did not. On the other hand, we thought she could probably afford to buy half his share, so we decided it was only fair to consider the possibility of a joint purchase. The three of us consulted an Estes Park lawyer about the various options, and during our discussion in his office, the conversation turned to the ultimate disposition of the property. I mentioned in passing that because I was the only owner with a spouse or children, it appeared the property would eventually pass to my children. Diane immediately took offense at my remark and announced angrily that she would rather leave her share of the property to friends than to any of her relatives. Her attitude shocked me because it seemed so inconsistent with the wishes of my parents, who would unquestionably want the property to pass undivided to their grandchildren.

While Wells, Diane, and I were discussing that evening the possibility of buying Kent's share, she for some reason started telling me all the ways I had annoyed her during the past dozen years. It was a list of grievances that seemed minor, almost trivial, to Wells and me but obviously had assumed a great importance in her mind. She complained that when we put our children to bed at night, they didn't always stay there but sometimes came wandering back out to the living room. It seemed an odd complaint since her own extreme fear of the dark as a child had created a constant burden upon Mom. Diane also asserted that I was always telling her what to do. She reminded me that I had told her how to scrub the floor, an incident that I remembered well. One day when I had noticed her washing the kitchen floor with only five inches of water in the pail, I had tactfully suggested that she should use a full pail of water. She had responded angrily and had harbored that resentment all these years.

It was hard not to give Diane advice. Her mismanagement of Dad's affairs was painfully evident. One January when the metals prices had risen a little, I suggested we should sell enough to cover the tax bills due in April. Diane snapped back, "Don't tell me how to run my business!" But on the evening of April 14 she called me up to ask, "Where are we going to get the money to pay the taxes?" When I then asked her if she had sold a railroad bond of Dad's that she had already held for a couple of years past maturity, she replied she would do so soon. Three years later the bond still had not been sold, and we had lost $600 in interest.

The conversation that night in the cabin was extremely unpleasant. Diane finally said in cold and measured tones, "I have very little love left for you, Alison, even if you are my sister." As her bitter words died away, I felt in a sickening rush that all those years of childhood when we were such close companions were gone forever. Her icy declaration marked a turning point in our relationship and influenced many future decisions that Wells and I were to make.

This episode fell into an unfortunate pattern that had developed in Diane's life. She had always been a person with an intense need for affection and close human relationships. Diane demanded a great deal from a relationship, however, and when it did not live up to her high expectations, she was resentful. Mom had often commented on this tendency, saying, "Diane just writes people off."

In the letter Diane had sent to Mark in New Zealand, she complained that he did not love Mom and Dad enough. It is clear from the letter, however, that she was also very hurt that he didn't love her enough. Kent and she had been particularly close, but after his alcoholic problems became severe, she to a large extent gave up on him. Only recently she had virtually ended a very close, but platonic, relationship with a man with whom she shared a piano studio, a relationship that had lasted almost fourteen years.

When Aunt Thelma was eighty-eight years old and as kind and alert as ever, Diane severed all contact with her because she felt Aunt Thelma didn't offer her sufficient sympathy. It was particularly ironic because Aunt Thelma was by that point the person who loved Diane the most, patiently overlooking or putting up with all her eccentricities. For several years, Aunt Thelma had spent July with us in the main cabin and August with Diane, which was important for Diane, who didn't like to be alone in the cabin.

A particularly unfortunate incident occurred the summer after Diane had broken with Aunt Thelma. Aunt Thelma was visiting Wells and me, and Diane drove up with a friend to use the upper cabin for a night. I kept expecting Diane to come down to the main cabin to get some sheets to use, but she had obviously brought her own along in order to avoid seeing us. The next morning Aunt Thelma, Wells, and I were eating breakfast in the kitchen, which looked out on the driveway, as Diane and her friend started to load the car to return to Denver. We kept hoping that Diane would come inside to say hello to Aunt Thelma, but it was not to happen. I will never forget the image of the tears rolling down Aunt Thelma's cheeks when she saw the car drive off and knew that Diane had deliberately refused to see her.

Diane was not at all close to Dad, never inviting him to visit her in Denver or Estes Park and rarely visiting him in Palisade. It was admittedly difficult to have him visit at Estes Park, but he loved to spend time there with the family. It hardly seemed fair to exclude him from the property when he had paid for it. During the years Mom lived in Colorado, Diane always invited Mom for Christmas but never Dad. Of course, Mom felt less relaxed when Dad was around, but it was sad to think of Dad always spending Christmas alone when he was only a few hours away. Diane blamed him so much for not being a better husband to Mom that she did not always appreciate his good qualities. Once she shocked me by saying in front of Kathryn, who was only twelve at the time, that Dad had purchased the Estes Park property so that he could have peace and quiet at home for the summer without the rest of us. Nothing could be more unfair to Dad. For all his faults, he was a self-effacing person and was genuinely happy to see the rest of us escape every summer from the sweltering Nebraska heat to enjoy the Colorado mountains.

Thus Diane had in effect withdrawn from all of us but Mom, and Mom she had virtually lost because of her mental problems. For Diane, with her deep need for affection, it was a personal tragedy.

The Krotter lumberyard in Palisade in the late 1890s. The wooden building in the left center was later replaced by a large brick building.

F.C. (Fred) and Nellie Krotter's wedding picture.

Nellie Krotter in front of her Palisade home.

F.C. and Nellie Krotter with their sons Dean and Chauncey.

F.C. (Fred) Krotter

Dean, Nellie, and
Chauncey Krotter

The Krotter home ("town house") in Palisade, Nebraska, circa 1980.

Interior of the Krotter home, circa 1915.

Audrey Musick Krotter,
circa 1919.

First Musick home in Summerfield, Kansas, circa 1911.

Second Musick home in Summerfield, Kansas, circa 1918. Audrey Musick Krotter is the girl in the center with long hair. To the left is her sister, Thelma; on the far left is her brother, Max. Oscar Musick is the man in the black hat, and Edmee Musick is the woman on the far right.

Oscar Musick's general store in Summerfield, Kansas, circa 1915.

Audrey Musick Krotter's
engagement picture.

Dean Krotter's engagement picture.

Dean and Audrey Musick Krotter's home (the "south house") on a farm just south of Palisade.

Main Street in Palisade, circa 1930. The building on the left was the Krotter hardware store.

Edmee and Oscar Musick with Diane and Kent Krotter.

Oscar and Edmee Musick's home on the Krotter farm just south of Palisade.

Kent Krotter on our pony on our farm just south of Palisade. Our garage, house, and chicken house appear in the background. The photo was taken from the yard of Oscar and Edmee Musick's home.

The Krotter cabin site in Estes Park, Colorado.

Trees bordering the creek on the Krotter farm south of Palisade.

Kent Krotter

Diane Krotter's high school graduation picture.

Alison Krotter Johnson's college graduation picture.

Wells and Alison Krotter Johnson's wedding picture taken in the front yard of the Estes Park cabin.

The Methodist Church in Palisade built by the Krotter family in 1954.

Thelma Musick

Mark Krotter

Margaret Yates and Mark Krotter's wedding picture.

Audrey Musick Krotter

Dean Krotter

Helen and Clark Brown

Main Street in Palisade, Nebraska, circa 1980.

The "south house" as it appeared in 1978 with its crumbling back steps when we returned to Nebraska to search for the gold and silver.

Oscar and Edmee Musick's house on our farm as it appeared in 1978.

The side yard of the "town house" in the 1930s. The brick garage on the left is where Dean Krotter buried a large wooden box of silver coins in a back room with a dirt floor.

Alison Krotter Johnson and Wells Johnson at an alpine lake in Rocky Mountain National Park near Estes Park.

Dear Sirs;

I am now on the eighth lesson of your Yogism Course. How much improvement should the average student show at this point? I know that this is rather hard to judge but could you give me at least a rough estimate?

The eighth lesson is two lesson past the half-way point of the course but I do not feel that I have travelled that far toward the rewards promised. I have noticed some changes such as a more detached attitude, better grades, more endurance, and perhaps greater concentration. These improvements, however, are so subtle and so subject to retrogressions that I sometimes wonder whether they are really worth the large amount of money, time and effort which I have put in on this course so far. Indeed, I sometimes wonder whether these improvements exist at all.

From the first lesson the time spent on Yogism has increased from the "15 minutes a day" until, at the present time, I am spending over two hours a day. The circumstances are not of the best, either, as I am attending college and am living in a dormatory. It is necessary that I get up before five o'clock every morning in order that I may carry on my Yogism work at a time when I will not be disturbed by my roommate or other students and at a time which will be the same every day and which will allow me to do the exercise all at once.
I only mention these facts to show that I am trying and to justify my belief that I should be making greater progress. I will consider the money, time, and effort all exceedingly well spent if I receive the promised benefits of this course. I However, would simply like to know how my development compares with the average. Please let me know. Thank you.

Yours truly

Ken t Krotter

and I intend to continue to do my best no matter what my progress seems to be.

Carbon copy of the letter Kent Krotter sent to the company offering a "yogism" course.

Vault 44-A

Coffee Can #174

	Quarters, single	596 quarters
	Canadian quarters, single	5 Canadian quarters
many B.U. dimes	Dimes, single	430 dimes
	Nickels, single	1298 nickels

Coffee Can #175 (orange)

	Nickels, single	1196 nickels
	Quarters, single	662 quarters
	Canadian quarters, single	2 Canadian quarters
	Dimes, single	408 dimes

Sanilac Bottle #176 (medium)

Bottom	Nickels, single	318 nickels
Middle	Quarters, single	292 quarters
	Canadian quarters	2 Canadian quarters
Top	Dimes, single	187 dimes
	Canadian dimes, single	1 Canadian dime

Coffee Can #177 (red folger's)

| Most apparently B.U. | Quarters, $10 rolls with 40 per roll | 17 rolls |

1961 P (8 rolls)
1954 S (4 rolls)
1954 D (2 rolls)
1954 P (1 roll)
-Unidentified (1 roll)

Page 62 of Diane Krotter's inventory from hand counting the coins.

OCTOBER 18, 1982

TO MY DEAR CHILDREN--MARK, KENT, DIANE AND (ALISON;)
    TODAY I HAVE ACQUIRED A LARGE AMOUNT OF 100 OUNCE ENGELHARD
SILVER BARS AND WISH TO GIVE EACH OF YOU 31 — OF THESE SILVER
BARS. THESE BARS COST ME $978.00 (978.00) EACH, SO THE TOTAL AMOUNT GIFTED
TO EACH OF YOU IS $ 30,318.00

    I WISH TO TRANSFER THESE BARS TO EACH OF YOU CHILDREN BECAUSE
THEY ARE JUST TOO HEAVY FOR ME TO CARRY AROUND IN MY PURSE!

    I ALSO WISH TO EXERCISE PART OF MY UNIFIED CREDITS AGAINST MY
ESTATE TAX LIABILITY IN ORDER TO GIVE YOU THESE SILVER BARS, AND
THUS TRANSFER THESE TO YOU AT MY COST ON THIS DATE.

    I HOPE THAT SOME DAY THIS GIFT WILL BRING YOU MUCH HAPPINESS
AND FOND MEMORIES.

LOVE, YOUR MOTHER,

Audrey Krotter

AUDREY N. KROTTER

Letter that Audrey Musick Krotter was given to sign to accompany
the silver bars she gave her children.

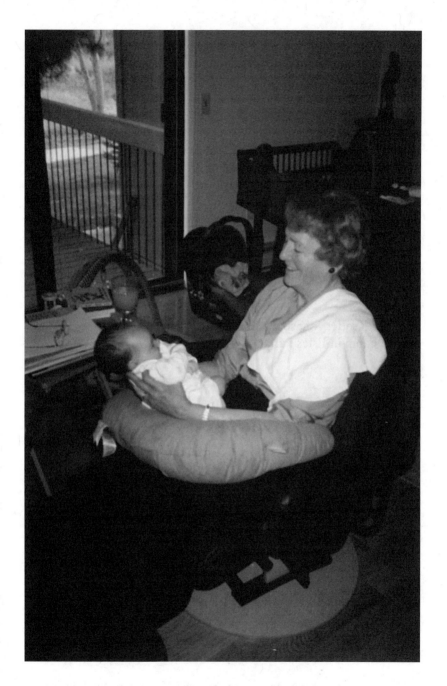

Alison Krotter Johnson and her grandson.

Alison Krotter Johnson building an extra bedroom onto the upper guest cabin in Estes Park.

The arrow marks the location of the land Alison Krotter Johnson sold to Tom Dreiss. View from the back terrace of the cabin.

CHAPTER TWENTY

The Estes Park property was the real family treasure. Wells and I decided to go ahead and purchase Kent's share of it by ourselves so that as much of the property as possible would eventually pass to our daughters. We called Kent to make him an offer, which he accepted. The deal would have probably gone through had he not asked if we could telegraph the money at once. That was most surprising because I had sent him the $3,000 from Mom only three weeks earlier. When I asked why he needed money so quickly, he hesitated and then said it wasn't he who needed money immediately but a very good friend of his. I could see that strange things were going on back in Ohio, so I made it clear that the money wouldn't change hands until we drew up the deed and arranged all the legal matters. Since the whole situation was highly suspicious, Wells and I decided that we should get more information before proceeding.

Over the next few days we learned more and more sordid details about Kent's life. First he explained that the friend who needed the money was a compulsive gambler to whom he had already lent a few thousand dollars. Meanwhile, as the phone calls came in, Mom sat anxiously wringing her hands, guessing there was a problem with either Kent or Dad. At one point she said to us, "Don't tell me what it is; I don't want to know." Since she happened to be in a rather low and depressed mood already, we had no intention of relating to her the appalling things we were hearing.

We asked Kent if there were other people living in his house because someone else often answered the phone. He replied that a woman named Elizabeth lived with him, together with her eighteen-year-old son. The next phone call we received was from Kent's gambler friend, Harry Richardson. We were not favorably disposed toward him, but his phone call disarmed us somewhat because he was a very intelligent, articulate person and seemed interested in Kent's welfare. He confirmed that Kent was again drinking heavily and had been unemployed for some time. Harry assured us that although he had borrowed money from Kent in the past and had not yet repaid the debt, he had his welfare at heart and often had provided him with meals when he didn't have enough to eat. He thought it was important to get Kent to "take the cure" at this point. It was a puzzling phone call; we weren't sure what to make of Harry Richardson. The next night we received a call from Kent, with Harry joining the conversation on an extension phone. Harry had persuaded Kent to explain to us all about his friend Elizabeth. It was a shocking and depressing tale. Kent had met her at a mental health clinic where he was being treated for alcoholism and she for manic-depression. We later heard she was many years older than Kent. She first moved in with him when he was still living in an apartment. Kent was very reluctant to tell us the sordid details and was clearly intoxicated. He began by saying, "I really hate to say this; it's really difficult for me to tell you these things." Then he described how Elizabeth had deliberately set fire to his apartment. The fact that Kent didn't immediately get rid of her after that disaster told me how hopeless it was to try to patch together his life. Before long she attempted suicide in his apartment via the gas oven. He arrived home just in time to save her; the emergency room doctor said she would have died if he had been any later.

During this period, Kent had bought a new house that turned out to be only an albatross around his neck. It was a large old brick house with two main floors and a usable attic. Kent thought he was getting a bargain, but it was the kind of house that needed lots of expensive repairs. He had bought it without checking carefully enough into the costs of making it livable. The previous plumbing and hot-water heating system had frozen, breaking several pipes and radiators, so the entire system had to be redone.

Kent's large house had made it all too attractive for Elizabeth to move in, bringing her teenage son along. He seemed to be a problem almost equal to his mother. Kent, who loved to indulge in amateur psychology, told us that he diagnosed him to be a "psychopath." Whatever the reasons were for Kent making that evaluation, it was obvious he should never have let the boy past the front door. As it turned out, he stole some gold coins from Kent. Like his father, Kent had purchased a number of gold coins but didn't believe banks were a safe place to keep them because of the danger of government confiscation. As I later learned, the ironic part of the whole episode was that he had spent $3,000 on an elaborate fire and burglar alarm system to protect his gold.

Only Kent would spend $3,000 on a burglar alarm system and then invite a thief to live with him.

When Diane and I heard this sorry tale, we told Kent that he was never going to get his life together unless he got rid of these strange characters. He agreed but assured us that Elizabeth was no longer a problem because she had inherited a little money from her ex-husband and was now living in a small town some twenty miles away. But in the next breath, Kent told us that Elizabeth was temporarily staying in his house because her sister was dying of cancer in a nearby hospital. That sounded highly suspicious; I suspected Elizabeth was maintaining contact with him in hopes of getting more money. He said he had lent her a couple of thousand, but the amount was probably much larger. Of course, I wondered why he hadn't asked her to repay the debt from her recent inheritance.

The next night we received a phone call from Harry, who wanted to talk to us while Kent was not present. He told us that Elizabeth was an awful person. As an example, he described how she had once poured a bottle of salad oil over Kent's head. Harry underlined his annoyance with Elizabeth and her son by saying that at one point he had brought in the police to get them out of Kent's house. Then he told us that he had gone out to California to take a job but had heard that Elizabeth and her son had moved back in with Kent in his absence. He had dropped everything and returned to Ohio to oust them once more from Kent's house. That puzzled us. Why would Harry go to such lengths to try to keep Elizabeth and her son out of Kent's life? The most likely explanation was that both Harry and Elizabeth were after Kent's money, and each didn't want the other cutting in on his or her territory. At any rate, Harry viewed Elizabeth as a continuing problem, despite Kent's assertion that he was going to have nothing more to do with her.

Harry also told us where most of Kent's money had gone. As part of the conservatorship business, we had paid off the balance of the inheritances due to the Krotter grandchildren from their grandmother. Kent had received about $50,000 only a couple of years earlier. It was hard to imagine how he had gone through so much money so quickly since he had made only a small down payment on his house, but Harry explained that Kent had lost a large sum playing the silver futures market and had also invested in bogus emeralds.

Harry had originally met Kent because Elizabeth's son had offered to sell to Harry the gold coins he had stolen from Kent. Becoming suspicious and learning the boy lived with Kent, Harry called to ask if Kent were missing any coins. Although it appeared that Harry was helping Kent out in this case, he probably viewed Kent as fertile territory for future con-operations and was simply attempting to ingratiate himself with him. We later learned that Kent had shown Harry the inventory of Dad's gold and silver hoard that Diane had sent him. It must have seemed the answer to any con-man's prayers.

According to Harry, Kent's house was such a pigsty and smelled so foul it was hard for him to go there. Kent had a cat but kept no litter-box for it, so cat feces and urine on the floors added to the mess throughout the house. Harry also reported that Kent had sold most of his furniture to raise money and was sleeping on the floor in a corner.

On previous occasions Harry had taken Kent to the city drying-out center for a few days, and he was trying to persuade him to go there now. I urged Kent to return to Hazelden in Minnesota for extended treatment, assuring him that Mom would be willing to pay the bill. He was adamant about not returning there, however. I spent hours on the telephone seeing if I could locate a good facility in California, where Kent preferred to go, but long-term facilities there were available only for California residents.

We remained puzzled about Harry. It wasn't clear that he had any occupation. Kent told us he was sort of an entrepreneur, which in retrospect we should have interpreted to mean "con-man." Kent kept talking about what a wonderful friend Harry was and told us that it was the first time in his life he had really had a friend. When we questioned his lending so much money to him, he replied, "Harry is such a good friend he would rather kill himself than not be able to repay me." It was hopeless trying to deal with that kind of naïveté.

Another day Harry called to say that he had once taken Kent to Las Vegas when Kent had been feeling depressed because he thought the trip would cheer Kent up. Later on Kent decided to make a return trip by himself. After a few days, Harry became concerned about him and called some of the hotels. He learned that Kent had passed out at the roulette wheel and had been returned to his room in a wheelchair by the hotel management. Harry flew out to Las Vegas to bring Kent home before all his money could disappear.

With Kent in such a precarious financial state that creditors might obtain a hold over our Colorado property, it was important to settle at once the question of a possible purchase of his share of the cabin. Wells and I finally decided it would be safest to include Diane in a joint purchase effort because we didn't want to bid against her with Kent in such an alcoholic fog that he might grab at any offer if he could get his hands on the cash quickly enough. We realized full well, however, that if we sent him a large sum of money for the land, it would be almost immediately lost. The only question would be how the vultures would divide it.

CHAPTER TWENTY-ONE

We were soon juggling not one family problem but two. Dad had become concerned about some farm land he owned in eastern Nebraska and had decided to take the bus to Omaha to investigate. When his housekeeper called me to ask if she should let him go, I said that if she couldn't talk him out of going, there wasn't much we could do to stop him. After spending a couple of days trying to arrange for Kent to take the cure, I decided I had better try to track Dad down. I called a hotel in Omaha, where he had stayed once the previous year. The clerk reported that Dad had spent one night there. Finally I located him in a small town hotel. When I mentioned that I had traced him to the hotel in Omaha, he told me he had stayed there only one night because it was too expensive. The next night he had slept outside in a small park near the motel. I wondered what the family was coming to, with Kent sleeping on the floor and Dad sleeping in a park. When I insisted to Dad that he couldn't sleep in parks, he just laughed at me. I had decided by now, however, that we had to take some chances in order for him to enjoy living in his own home. We could have avoided this kind of incident only by getting a guardianship and locking him up in a nursing home for the rest of his life.

Meanwhile, my phone calls to locate Dad were interspersed with more telephone reports from Ohio. Harry had managed to get Kent into a city detoxification center, where he stayed for several days. Now that Kent was temporarily sober, the two of them had a talk and had come up with a proposal. They wanted to use the money from Kent's share of Estes Park to set up a used trailer business. The affair could not have appeared more dubious had Kent proposed buying the Brooklyn Bridge. He told us that Harry had set up two other people in the used trailer business and they had each made $100,000 the first year. Kent's gullibility was beyond belief. Somehow he never quite got the picture that one had to work to make money. During our long phone conversation about his plan, I asked him why he thought he would like to run a used trailer business. I couldn't imagine a less likely occupation for him. Kent kept saying that he had always had problems before because he had no purpose in life, but now he would have something to live for. His assertion seemed yet another tragic-comic event in the ongoing Krotter saga. When I asked Kent why running a used trailer business would give him a purpose in life, he kept coming back to the huge profit potential. I asked him why making $100,000 would supply his life with meaning, but he didn't see my point. Something queer and distorted was operating deep within his personality, impelling him to seek self-justification through making a large sum of money. Perhaps he had still not outgrown his youthful need to impress his father and thus win his approval.

At any rate, the used trailer scheme left us with no doubts about Harry; we were dealing with a con-man and a very smooth one at that. Hence we became even more concerned about the Estes Park property. Although Kent himself was in no condition to find a purchaser outside the family, Harry was clearly a sharp operator. He might help Kent arrange a sale to a real estate agent or someone else who would buy the property as a speculation. We discussed this possibility with Raymond Hanson, who finally volunteered to go out to Ohio as the family's legal representative to advise us about the Estes Park purchase. Before he left, Raymond told us he was sure Harry was a con-man.

But after his trip, Raymond decided that Kent should have his chance and that it was all right for us to buy his share of Estes Park to enable him to enter the used trailer business with Harry. When I asked Raymond about the financial details of the used trailer business, I was amazed to learn that they had not discussed those questions. His impression of Harry had been favorable, but he said, "It does seem strange to me that Harry would bestow his friendship in such a way." Raymond later said he had seen many alcoholics in his lifetime, but never one like Kent.

Diane and I both told Raymond we still thought the whole used trailer idea was a con-operation, and we in no way wanted to back it. I was both surprised and angry that a sophisticated lawyer like Raymond would let himself be conned along with Kent, especially since we had paid for his trip to Ohio. After some further thought, however, we decided that it was just too risky to leave Kent's share of Estes Park dangling, so we made him a joint offer that he accepted with our added proviso that $10,000 of the purchase price would go directly from us to his creditors.

While we were negotiating the Estes Park purchase, Harry was passing along disquieting information, probably all true, that Kent was planning to invest part of the proceeds in the silver futures market. This was particularly alarming because he could lose money faster in silver futures than in almost any other investment.

One night about two weeks after we had closed the Estes Park sale, Wells and I were awakened at 1 A.M. by a phone call from Harry. He had set up a conference call with Diane and me to tell us he was thinking about instituting breach of promise proceedings against Kent. He said that during their conversation with Raymond, Kent had made a commitment to go into the used trailer business. Of course, Kent could have made no final commitment because he had no money at that point. Harry told us, however, that on the basis of that supposed commitment, he had promised to rent a vacant lot for the business. Now Kent was debating whether he wanted to go into the used trailer business, and Harry said this indecision left him in an awkward position. When I asked if he had signed a lease on the lot, he said he had not, so I suggested there was no problem. He replied that he had made a verbal commitment and felt obligated to the amount of $5,000. I said he had been rash to make any commitment with no money in hand from Kent and the whole idea still in the speculative stage. I further asserted that I couldn't see how he could take legal action against Kent on this basis anyway because he owed Kent several thousand dollars. When Harry realized that I knew of his debt to Kent, he began backing down on his threats to sue. Probably the whole purpose of the phone call was to see if he could milk us for $5,000 by his threats. At least the call laid to rest any doubts about whether Harry was a con-man.

As we were winding up our conversation, Harry suddenly blurted out, "Another thing you should know is that Kent is going around showing everyone this list of all the gold and silver your family owns." We had asked Raymond to remind Kent in Harry's presence that he was not an heir to his father's estate, so that Harry wouldn't have mistaken ideas about Kent's potential worth. This new knowledge was undoubtedly the reason Harry sounded so angry when he mentioned the list: he was dismayed to learn that Kent would never inherit any of the gold and silver.

Although Kent was not an heir to Dad's estate, he was of course still included in Mom's will. That fall she was well enough to visit us in New England, and it was a joy to see her something of her old self again. Diane and I had decided that we should now tell her about Kent's current problems, and we suggested that she leave his share of her eventual estate in trust, so that it would not be dissipated. Agreeing this was the best course, she made a new will when she returned to Colorado.

CHAPTER TWENTY-TWO

In the fall of 1981, Dad started legal action to lift the conservatorship. During the last few years, he had been very unhappy to see others managing his business affairs, and now he had recovered sufficient strength to fight to regain control. Two lawyers rejected him before he found one, Gerald Smith, who agreed to take his case. Mr. Smith arranged to have Dad interviewed and tested by a psychologist, who reported he found him knowledgeable about economics and capable of managing his own affairs. This evaluation alarmed us because Dad's memory and judgment were so obviously faulty. Anyone who would sleep in a city park when he had plenty of money was hardly competent to manage his own affairs. Although Dad could still talk very intelligently about economic matters, his memory was patchy, and he no longer remembered having sold various businesses and plots of land. He often became angry that he was not receiving rent on land he had sold long ago.

But our greatest fear was that if Dad regained control of his property, he would move the coins back to Palisade and hide them once again. He had no idea of the enormous size of his hoard because Diane had concealed all information about it from him. But he knew that there were some coins stored in a bank, and he insisted he wanted them back home. After all the effort we had expended to locate the hoard and move it out in the first place, it was nightmarish to think that we might have to do it all over again some day. It would have been like running a movie backwards, with the gold and silver all streaming back onto the cupboard shelves and into the holes in the ground. We were also worried because Dad was no longer discreet about his affairs. If he did move the metals back, everyone in town would soon know all about it, and there would be a great risk of robbery and physical harm to him.

Meanwhile, Dad was having health problems. Despite prolonged efforts, I had not been able to talk him into having his old coal furnace replaced by an oil burner. When the coal furnace malfunctioned in late February, filling the house with smoke, he became ill from smoke inhalation and was hospitalized. His doctor decided that Dad's irregular heart rhythm necessitated a pacemaker and recommended that the operation be done in either Denver or Kearney, Nebraska. Denver was obviously the most convenient place to have it done, and I said I would go out to handle all the details since Diane had had most of the burden of caring for Mom. While I was making arrangements to fly to Denver, I received a call from Dad's doctor saying he refused to go to Denver for the operation. I finally said I would go on out to Imperial, Nebraska, where Dad was hospitalized, and try to talk him into going to Denver. Diane decided to go out to Nebraska with me since we both were afraid he might die at any moment.

After I arrived at the airport, I called Dad's housekeeper to check in. She said that the hospital had just called to ask her to come and get Dad because he was very upset and was shouting at everyone that he was not going to Denver for the operation but was just going to go home. His doctor finally decided to let him leave so he wouldn't have a heart attack on the spot.

Diane and I arrived in Palisade late that night and talked to Dad about the operation, but he was adamant about not going to Denver. He had always wanted to die in Nebraska, partly because of personal loyalty to the state, but also because of a mistaken idea that his will might be probated in Colorado if he died there. Diane, unfortunately, was equally adamant that he should have the operation in Denver because that was more convenient for the rest of us. She was understandably tired after all the years she had been burdened with parental problems. On the other hand, I believed that if Dad felt he was close to death, he ought to have a say in where he was going to die. He reminded me of Dylan Thomas's old man, not about to "go gentle into that good night." I could see that I would just have to go with him to have the operation done in Kearney, so the next morning I told Dad I would take him there. We made the arrangements and left a few hours later. Dad's doctor had set up the operation for late that afternoon, thinking he might die at any moment.

We stopped to eat lunch in McCook at Dad's favorite restaurant that served a buffet he considered to be a great bargain. Dad was always a very slow eater, and on this occasion he laboriously ate his way through a large plate of food, despite my protestations that we needed to get him to the hospital in Kearney right away. At last we got on the road once again. As we drove along the sparsely traveled country roads of central Nebraska, up and down the brown and treeless rolling hills that did not yet show any sign of the approaching spring, I kept wondering what thoughts were going through Dad's mind as he faced the possibility of death at any moment. His thoughts were clearly on death, for as we entered Kearney, he said to me, "Tell all my friends in Palisade good-bye for me."

Fortunately, the operation was a success, and I was able to take Dad home within a few days. After I drove him back to Palisade, I was so tired that I went upstairs to rest a while before I would have to leave that night. In a few minutes, I heard Dad climbing slowly up the stairs; he came into my room and sat down in a rocking chair to talk to me. I knew he felt so lonely living there all by himself that he didn't want to miss the chance to spend all the time he could with me before I once again disappeared from his life. As he rocked slowly back and forth, he started telling me about various incidents from the past and said to me with tears in his eyes, "Dad and Mother were very proud when I married Audrey; they thought I had made a very good choice." I sighed to myself to see how dependent he still was upon his parents' opinion after all these years.

Even after his operation, Dad continued his attempt to overthrow the conservatorship. By now his lawyer, Gerald Smith, realized Dad wasn't competent, but he didn't know how to handle the awkward situation. Finally, Raymond Hanson and Gerald agreed that they would ask to have a court-appointed visitor go out to Palisade to interview Dad and various people around town. The visitor would then make a recommendation to the court. This plan was implemented in April, and the visitor agreed with the rest of us that Dad wasn't competent. Fortunately, Dad soon passed out of his combative mood and let the matter drop. Mr. Smith had probably pointed out to him that in the light of the visitor's report, he had little chance of regaining control of his hoard of gold and silver.

CHAPTER TWENTY-THREE

That May of 1982 we received a letter from Jack Harrington, the Ohio coin dealer whom Kent had told all about the hoard. He proposed we convert our great volume of silver coins into silver bars because in times of sharp price increases in silver, the price of silver coins starts to lag substantially behind the bullion price. The profit in "junk" silver coins is not ultimately realized until they are melted down. In late January of 1980, when the tremendous price jump to $48 an ounce occurred, the smelters were backed up for months. Purchasers had to hedge their bets, trying to guess where the price of silver might be a few months hence. At the time I was offered twenty-four times face for our junk silver coins, the actual melt value was thirty-six times face.

As Wells and I studied the proposal, we could see a great deal of merit in this conversion, which would change a large mass of coins that were cumbersome to market into a stack of silver bars that could be quickly sold at advantageous prices in the event of another price surge. Since silver had by now dropped to around $8 an ounce, it seemed a particularly propitious time to make a conversion, with a fair prospect of later price increases.

I called Jack and had a long discussion with him. He said he was going to be in Colorado on business at the end of June anyway and could at least appraise the hoard for us. We clearly needed to have a better idea of the value of the various coins in order to manage the hoard effectively, and his appraisal rate was $50 an hour, far lower than Charles Stack's rate had been.

We had some serious discussions with Diane about the subject. Two years earlier I had opposed the plan to use Jack, but the idea of converting from junk coins to silver bars seemed to have much more merit than his previous suggestion of converting into rare coins. I was still concerned that he had been recommended by Kent, but I was willing to admit that that fact alone should not damn him. It did not seem quite ethical to me to act upon Jack's conversion proposal by going to another dealer because it would not have occurred to us to take such a step at this time had we not received his letter. The day would soon come, however, when I greatly regretted that attention to a fine point of morality had helped put us into Jack's hands. Since Diane refused to use a local appraiser and seemed to like Jack, we decided to hire him to appraise the hoard, with the idea that we would then give further thought to the conversion possibility.

Several days before we were all about to converge on Denver in late June, I suggested to Diane that because the proposal of converting the silver coins to silver bars was based on the assumption that the bulk of what we had was in fact junk silver, we should try to check that out before Jack arrived. By taking a representative sample of the silver coins to a coin dealer or two in Denver, she could check on their general quality. In particular, we had found a great many very shiny dimes in the garage cache that might carry an extra premium. Unfortunately, Diane's only response was to say, "I had the collection all arranged and inventoried and you came in and moved it around, so I'm not going to attempt to find anything now." She said it in such an angry tone of voice that it was useless to pursue the discussion, but I ceded the point with great reluctance. Yet again it was extremely frustrating to see Diane totally mishandle matters that had such enormous consequences for my future inheritance.

Jack arrived in Denver in late June on the same day we flew in for the summer. Diane and I had agreed we would share the job of assisting Jack in the vaults so that there was always a family member present. She was now able to sign a card giving me access to the vaults without her.

Once again I spent long hours in the vaults, listening to the endless rhythmical clinking of a coin counter. Jack ran our bags through a machine again, pulling out some Canadian silver and a few nonsilver nickels that his ear could detect by the slightly different ring they made when falling into the bag of nickels. As we were running the dimes through the counter, I asked Jack if there might not be a premium on the shiny dimes. He assured me there wasn't, and with him on the spot it was difficult to get a second opinion without implying that we questioned his integrity.

The first day that I worked with Jack I was at a loss to know what I thought about him. I neither instinctively trusted him, nor did I feel I had any real grounds yet for questioning his integrity. My conclusion was that we should proceed very cautiously in any deals with him. That evening I called Raymond Hanson to express my sense of uneasiness and to ask what his impression of Jack had been after meeting him that morning. He commented that he thought Jack was a rather brash young man. It was most unfortunate that within a few months Raymond would let this brash young man talk him into disastrous moves. We had all been surprised to learn that Jack was only in his late twenties. I expressed my concern to Raymond that we might find ourselves in a shell game, exchanging one thing for another without being sure we were getting a fair trade.

After I had spent a couple of days working with Jack, Diane relieved me, and I joined Wells and the children at the cabin. A few days later I received a call from Diane saying that Jack and she would like to drive up with Mom so that we could all five have a conference about the coins. Diane said they were busy typing up contracts for having Jack convert the coins to silver bars. I replied that it seemed premature to be typing contracts when we had not yet decided on this conversion. Jack, however, was always two jumps ahead of us, pushing for fast action before anyone had time to analyze the situation.

After the three of them arrived at Estes Park, we all sat down to study Jack's proposals, now in contract form. Our discussions began with the possibility of using the silver bars that we would obtain through the conversion to pay off part of a debt of $221,000 that Dad owed to Mom. Over the years Dad had transferred various business interests to Mom for estate tax reasons. As profits came in, he used all the cash to buy more coins and made appropriate bookkeeping entries to credit her account and debit his. Mom had plenty of money without calling in the debt, and it was clear anyway that the metals were available if she ever did need them. We had previously seen no reason to pay this debt before Dad died because it would cost $40,000 to $50,000 in capital gains tax to use gold and silver to pay the debt and interest. This tax would not have to be paid if Dad predeceased Mom, which seemed highly likely.

On the other hand, if we decided that it made sense to convert the silver coins to bars, we would end up paying the capital gains tax anyway, so the silver bars could then be used to pay off the debt to Mom without incurring any further tax.

One idea under discussion was to then have Mom give away some of these bars to us children, a plan that seemed worth considering since it had long been apparent that most of the gold and silver would eventually pass to us anyway. One reason for doing this was that by now it was obvious that Diane and I disagreed radically about investing in precious metals. I believed that when prices were sufficiently advantageous to cover the capital gains tax of almost twenty percent and still offer substantial profit, we should sell a large portion of the hoard. Diane, on the other hand, viewed gold and silver not as instruments of investment but as objects of an almost religious veneration. Over these last few years she had developed the same miserly traits she had seen in Dad, turning to gold as a substitute for everything that was missing in her life. Only as a matter of absolute necessity did she ever sell metals out of the hoard. The option of shifting some of the silver from Dad to Mom and then to us would allow each of us to play the metals market as we saw fit.

That afternoon we discussed all these possibilities at length. Nothing was decided about how much, if any, Mom should give away if she did receive partial payment on the debt. By the end of the afternoon, we had more or less decided, however, to convert our junk silver coins into silver bars and to sell Jack our brilliant uncirculated silver dollars and also two hundred rolls of brilliant uncirculated nickels. These latter sales were probably the most dubious part of the deal. Jack convinced us that it was a good way of generating cash to pay the tax on our conversion from coins to bars. In retrospect, I can see it would have been wiser just to have used some of the junk silver coins to pay the tax. We had only Jack's word on the value of these brilliant uncirculated coins. Had I had the power to act independently, I would have gotten bids on the same items from a dealer or two in Denver. But as usual, I was stymied by Diane's adamant refusal to consult local coin dealers.

Jack was full of other ideas too. He kept suggesting we take all our circulated gold coins and trade them for brilliant uncirculated (B.U.) $20 gold coins. I continually vetoed that idea because we had no way of judging the value of the coins he would trade to us. This sort of horse trading could only benefit the expert, and that was Jack. Only a few weeks later I was amazed to receive from him a detailed proposal for just the opposite course of action: to take our B.U. gold coins and trade them for bullion-type coins. This sudden reversal alarmed me, but it didn't seem to bother Diane. Jack also said he thought we had too much gold and not enough silver in the estate. He suggested that at some point in the future Diane should exchange part of the gold for silver. Since this kind of exchange always generated a handsome profit for Jack, his constant and ever-changing proposals seemed highly dubious.

During the discussions it again became painfully apparent that Diane would not sell any of the gold or silver if the prices went up to an attractive level. Jack and she were still dreaming about unrealistic price increases, and it seemed certain that Diane's expectations that the price of gold would double or triple before many years passed would prevent her from ever selling at lower levels. Although Jack was not the philosophical gold-bug Diane was, he still had rosy ideas about the future of precious metals, and his influence on Diane was going to be all in the wrong direction.

Even after Jack had returned to Ohio with his signed contracts and handsome profit in hand, we had not heard the last of his ideas. I received frequent phone calls from him, as did Diane, and the more he talked, the more nervous I became. He even suggested flying over to Zurich to exchange some coins for us. In one phone conversation he said, "Gee, I just wish I could find another family like yours with all this gold and silver." I could hardly believe he would be so brash as to blurt that out. Another day he called to say, "Now we have to decide what we should do with your father's estate and your mother's estate." It was none of his business what we did with Dad and Mom's estates, and Wells and I were becoming more and more suspicious that Jack's proposals were merely an attempt to generate commissions for himself. Unfortunately, Diane did not share our suspicions, and she held the power.

CHAPTER TWENTY-FOUR

There were problems with the coins, there were problems with Mom. The day she left Fairview Terrace to come to the cabin in Estes Park she hurt her back lifting a suitcase, and this injury was very painful. She was again talking incessantly, and I began to wonder if her back difficulty was augmented by a recurring mental problem. Every day she had me drive her into town to visit a chiropractor, but she refused to consult a medical doctor.

Mom finally suggested it would be easiest for her to stay a few days at the motel adjacent to her chiropractor's office. I readily agreed because her deteriorating emotional state and nonstop talking were wearing us all down. Twelve years of dealing with her mental problems had left us virtually numb in such situations. The situation was particularly awkward at the moment because Wells's mother and niece were visiting us.

After Mom had been downtown a couple of days, she began to sound rather wild over the phone, so I drove down to check on her. When I asked if she was taking her lithium regularly, she assured me she was. To my further questions she replied, "Do you want me to swear it on the Bible?" as she went to the bedside stand to pull out the Gideon Bible. Pills scattered all over the floor of her motel room showed only too clearly her state of confusion. It was late afternoon by then, so I suggested we go over to the hospital emergency room to see if a doctor could check her back pain. I hoped to get her into the hospital, where she could be more easily handled. Fortunately, the doctor did suggest she be hospitalized for evaluation of the back problem. When he took a blood sample to check her lithium level, it turned out to be almost zero. This confirmed my belief that while Mom was ordinarily very honest, you could not rely upon her word that she was taking her lithium if she was already slipping mentally.

Mom failed so rapidly that within a couple of days she could not even walk unaided. She also began to give the hospital personnel a lot of trouble. When her doctor reported that she was very hostile and asked if that was her normal behavior, I assured him that was entirely out of character for Mom. Within a week or so, this hostility disappeared as her proper lithium level was reestablished, but she remained very debilitated. By now it was apparent we could not care for Mom at home, so Diane and I finally decided to put her in the nursing home wing of her retirement complex.

At the end of July, Wells and I drove Mom down to the nursing home at Fairview Terrace. Wells was unfailingly kind to Mom and did a great many things to help her in the absence of her sons. She was quite rational by this point but very discouraged to be entering the nursing home, even though she saw no viable alternative. I suggested that with physical therapy she might be able to become mobile again and return to her apartment, but I could tell she didn't believe me.

We still had not decided whether Mom should give us children any of the silver bars she was to receive from Dad. As this and many other questions involved Mark, I decided to see if I could get him to talk to me. Raymond Hanson had recently asked Mark's lawyer about a business matter, and to our surprise, Mark himself called Raymond to discuss the question. Now that we at last had his business phone number, I decided to try calling him. When he answered, I felt as if I were talking to someone returned from the dead. After discussing the questions involving Mom, I told him that Dad was very eager to see him and find out his opinion on various business matters. When I suggested that Dad would be very happy if Mark could fly down to Denver to meet with him for a little while sometime that summer, he replied, "I get along better with Dad when I don't see him." That seemed to sum up rather well Mark's approach to human relations.

After much thought about the question of gifts from Mom to us children, I came to a fairly conservative conclusion. Given her unpredictable mental condition and her recent bad period, it was all too clear that she could some day require care in a custodial mental home and this would be extremely expensive. It seemed prudent for her to make only $10,000 annual exclusion gifts to her four children, using $40,000 worth of bars and keeping $80,000 for herself.

Unfortunately, Mom's physical condition worsened rapidly in the nursing home, perhaps as a result of her negative attitude. I could understand, however, why she found the place depressing. Whenever we visited her, we could hear a cacophony of sounds from the hall. One patient kept up a constant chant of "Take me to the bathroom, take me to the bathroom." Another woman had a most unusual vocal protest. She would start wailing at a low pitch, and then her voice would rise gradually higher and higher. Then it slowly descended, all as she was being wheeled up and down the hall, so that the sound resembled an approaching and fading siren. The blackboard notices at the nurses' station provided occasional bits of humor, as on the day when someone wrote, "Herbert has lost his pants again."

Mom's roommate, Mrs. Robinson, was a lovely woman in her eighties who had to be wheeled about in a wheelchair. She was a frail, birdlike little creature, but even in her debilitated state, she radiated a beauty of character that was truly moving. Sometimes she would say to us as she sat in her wheelchair, "I'm so tired. Do you suppose you could ask one of the nurses to put me to bed, please?" One time I went out to the desk to ask someone to put her to bed, and the nursing supervisor said to me, "You know, all these patients would like just to crawl into bed and assume a fetal position, but if we let them, they would soon develop pneumonia and die." Their policy did not surprise me, but I wished they would just make poor Mrs. Robinson happy instead of worrying about her future.

CHAPTER TWENTY-FIVE

In mid-August, Diane and I made a trip down to Denver to consult with Raymond Hanson. We wanted to discuss the proposed transfer of the silver bars from Dad to Mom and the possibility of making annual exclusion gifts from Dad's estate to his three heirs.

The meeting turned out to be a crucial one. Before many minutes had elapsed, it was painfully apparent that Diane and Raymond would continue to drift along, subjecting the estate to incompetent management, never understanding the important economic and tax issues involved. Whenever I raised a tax planning question, Raymond shrugged his shoulders and said, "I'm not a tax lawyer." I wasn't a tax lawyer either, but I had studied enough books on estate planning to know that the one obvious thing to be done with a large estate like Dad's was to make annual exclusion gifts. Since Jack had just given us an appraisal figure for the gold and silver in the Denver vaults, we knew that there was about $600,000 worth of metals in Dad's estate. This meant we would be facing a heavy inheritance tax at his death. It therefore seemed reasonable to make three $10,000 gifts from Dad's estate to Diane, Mark, and me, thus moving $30,000 out of the estate tax-free and saving almost $10,000 in future taxes.

Raymond, however, said he wasn't sure that there was enough money to make those gifts. This seemed absurd. Dad only spent about $10,000 a year for his basic expenses and was in such a frail state of health it seemed unlikely he would live even three more years. We couldn't get Dad to spend money on anything anyway. He sweltered in 100-degree heat during Nebraska summers because he didn't want to pay for the electricity to run his air conditioner. With that kind of frugality, his money would easily outlast him.

This kind of estate planning seemed especially appropriate because Dad had always been very concerned about taxes. His plan had been that we children would just dig up the gold and silver at his death and divide it up without the government ever knowing anything about it, thus avoiding any estate tax. Our discussion of the gifts ended in an impasse, however, with Diane joining Raymond in questioning the advisability of making them. I was all for presenting the issue to the probate judge to let him decide since his predecessor on the bench had urged us to engage in this kind of estate planning. But neither of them wanted to try that route either.

Having made no progress on this issue, I raised another question. I believed we should immediately transfer the silver bars to Mom because we had already incurred the capital gains tax on the conversion from coins to bars. It was thus possible at last to pay off part of the debt from Dad to Mom without creating a further tax obligation. But with the price of silver rising steadily, we had to transfer the bars soon or we would incur a large additional tax on the increase in value since July. I could hold this silver for Mom under my existing power of attorney since it seemed clear she should not have immediate and unrestricted access to $120,000 worth of silver. Diane vetoed this idea also, making it clear she was afraid that I might sell some of the silver bars. She was undoubtedly alarmed by the possibility that control over that much silver might pass out of her hands.

Our discussion on these two issues that morning was so frustrating that I decided to broach the whole larger issue of the conservatorship. During the five years Diane had been conservatrix, I had become so impatient with her obvious mismanagement that I had often wished I were in charge of the estate. On one occasion when Diane had been complaining as usual at great length about all the work and trouble the conservatorship caused her, I had said, "If you would like to get out from under it, I would be glad to take over as conservatrix." She looked at me with fire in her eye and said in biting tones, "You'd love to get your hands on it, wouldn't you!"

During the last few weeks, Wells and I had decided the status quo was becoming intolerable. For five years we had watched Diane managing estate affairs with varying degrees of ineptness and losing hundreds of thousands through gross mismanagement of the gold and silver. We knew Diane well enough, though, to realize that if we suggested she step down or initiated any legal action against her, she would be mortally offended and leave none of her estate to our girls. Her growing animosity toward us and her emphatically stated intention not to leave the girls her share of Estes Park gave us little reason to believe, however, that she would leave them anything anyway, regardless of our actions. Therefore we decided to move to protect my future inheritance from Dad and Mom.

So it was that after the first fruitless hour of discussion that morning in Denver, I announced to Raymond and Diane that I thought that as a matter of justice and fairness, I should have a turn at being conservatrix because management of the estate affected all of our economic futures so greatly. Diane adamantly opposed this suggestion, however. It was apparent that she was very concerned that if I were in charge, I might sell some of the gold and silver. This was anathema to her.

Since Diane refused to consider the possibility of my being conservatrix, I suggested Dad's cousin, Bob Krotter, as an alternative. Dad had designated Bob as executor of his will, so the judge would have strong grounds for appointing him. But Diane didn't like that idea either.

I next suggested the following plan: we would set aside a substantial portion of Dad's estate to cover his potential needs and then divide the remainder into three parts. Each part would be assigned to one of Dad's heirs in a revocable trust. We would each manage the gold and silver in our trust as we saw fit. If Dad ever needed the money, the probate judge could revoke the trusts. On the other hand, if they were still in place at his death, each heir would receive what was in his or her respective trust.

Although this plan appeared to me to have much merit and to be inherently fair in letting Diane, Mark, and I each control our own future inheritance, Diane would not hear of it. Feeling increasingly frustrated and exasperated, I tried to get her to recognize the elementary justice of it. She, however, still refused to relinquish her hold on the conservatorship, and I began to wonder about her motivation. She insisted that she was acting for the good of all the family. I replied that I wanted to be the judge of what was good for me and was no longer willing to watch her wipe out my eventual inheritance because she was unable to recognize a selling opportunity when it was staring her in the face. Our meeting ended in a stalemate.

Another reason that we were so reluctant to leave Diane running the estate was her growing absorption in astrology. During the last few years, she had joined an astrology club and frequently attended meetings. Nothing could be more alien to Wells and me than this kind of dabbling with the irrational. The books that Diane brought to Estes Park showed her fascination not only with astrology, but also with clairvoyance, ESP, reincarnation, and predicting the future. The only book that seemed appropriate was a volume titled *A Guide for the Perplexed*. Diane was now spending hours studying her astrology books and charts and relating everything in life to astrology. When several hapless tourists were killed by a boulder that tumbled down a Colorado mountainside into their bus, she wondered aloud to my aunt what the birth dates of the deceased had been. We were increasingly concerned that such attitudes would affect her business decisions. With my inheritance at risk, it was hardly amusing to contemplate a conservatrix sitting on a fortune in gold and silver, making her decisions by the stars or fortune tellers.

One day in August when I had to go into the main cabin to walk Diane's dog, I happened to notice a sheet of paper lying on a kitchen chair. It probably only caught my eye because my name was printed in large letters across the top. The letters were spread out and under each was a number. These individual numbers were then added up to give another number, to the left of which was written the phrase "soul age." A few lines further down was my name written as my maiden name, with numbers again below the letters. It gave me a weird sensation to look at the paper; it was almost like finding a doll image of myself with pins stuck in it. It was so strange that I brought Wells down to see the paper for himself. For several months I wondered what the numbers meant. Then one day in a bookstore I had a chance to skim through a book on numerology. There was the phrase "soul age," defined to be a person's hidden, secret personality. This only confirmed my feeling that Diane's attitude toward me approached paranoia. Wells and I were more than ever convinced we had to remove her as conservatrix.

Many years later we saw an extreme example of Diane's tendency to approach various issues in a manner that was far from rational. In the late 1990s, she became very interested in the theory of "backward speech," which was being promoted by one of the talk radio programs to which she listens. According to the proponents of the "backward speech" theory, if you play backwards a tape recording of a person speaking, you can sometimes hear a secret message. Diane cited as examples that if you played one of President Clinton's statements about Monica Lewinsky backwards, you could heard the secret message, "I slept with her," and if you played backwards a statement by Joan Benet Ramsay's parents, you could hear the secret message, "We killed her."

CHAPTER TWENTY-SIX

After our pivotal meeting with Raymond Hanson, Diane and I stopped to see Mom on our way back to Estes Park. We were shocked by her condition. Since she had been eating almost nothing, she had become so weak that the few words she spoke were barely audible. She seemed hardly aware of our presence. Because her state was so alarming, we called her doctor as soon as we got back to Estes Park to ask him to visit her right away. He reported that her condition was indeed serious and said that she would probably die in a week or two if she didn't eat. It would be possible to hospitalize her and feed her through tubes, but he left that decision up to us. I told him Diane and I would talk the situation over and call him back. We discussed the matter only for a short while, for we knew that Mom would not want to be kept alive by unusual means. She had always made that clear. After Dad's heart attack in San Francisco, she had related to us how terrible it had been to see him struggling against the tubes they used to force-feed him in the hospital. Her life had not been easy since the onset of her mental problems some thirteen years before, and to prolong it by unpleasant means seemed cruel. While Diane and I were poles apart in most of our views, we both loved Mom very much and had no doubt that we were doing the right thing by letting her slip quietly away.

We called the doctor back to tell him our decision and then cried together at the thought that Mom would soon be gone. The time was particularly poignant because we were both thinking of what a wonderful person she had been in her prime and how frustrating her life had turned out to be. She had tried to be a good wife and mother, but now at the end of her life, she was faced with one son who appeared to be a hopeless alcoholic and another son who had not communicated with her in five years. The long years of recurring mental problems she had suffered had gradually taken their toll on her spirit and personality. Before her breakdown at age sixty-five, she had been a person of great vitality and interest in life, but these qualities had slowly been eroded by the traumatic emotional cycles that had plagued her since she became manic-depressive. It seemed terribly unfair that someone could be that nice and try that hard to do what was right and still end up with her life a shambles.

Diane and I decided to notify Kent, Mark, and Aunt Thelma to see if they wanted to come to be with Mom. We told Kent we would purchase his ticket from Mom's funds. Within a few days both Kent and Aunt Thelma flew out to Denver. When I called Mark, however, he indicated no interest in coming. I then urged him to call Mom or to at least send her flowers or even just a card. He did nothing, however, and his cold behavior seemed unforgiveable. Not only was Mom a very sweet person and a devoted mother, she had made it possible for Mark to receive a fine high school education at New Trier and she had encouraged him make the difficult move to Canada. She was the one who had to deal with the outrage expressed by people in Palisade when Mark went to Canada.

Diane and I returned to Fairview Terrace to be with Mom, who seemed to rally a little with our presence. When we fed her all her meals, she began to eat a little more and gained back some strength. Before long she was again talking, whereas a few days earlier she had been almost unable to articulate words.

When Kent arrived, Mom was so delighted she exclaimed, "Oh, Kent, I thought I would never see you again!" He spent a couple of weeks with her and was very good at feeding her and helping her in and out of bed. Aunt Thelma arrived shortly after Kent and stayed with her for almost two months. Her devotion contributed greatly to Mom's recovery.

I had a great love and admiration for Aunt Thelma, who "stuck by" those she loved through any adversity. On one occasion years earlier, I had found it very troubling to hear Kent say that while he loved Aunt Thelma, he regretted the fact that she would only engage in "small talk." Ironically enough, it was Aunt Thelma who had encouraged Mom to rent an apartment large enough for Kent to live with her when he was in the depths of his alcoholic problems so that Mom could take care of him. Aunt Thelma was not particularly interested in discussing philosophy, but she would never abandon a family member who needed help. There was nothing "small" about her.

When it was clear that the danger to Mom's health had passed, Diane and I went back up to Estes Park to spend a few days before closing the cabins. I made another call to Mark to say that Mom was now doing much better and had been delighted to see Kent. I told him that she would definitely know him if he could come now, but he did not make the trip, nor did he ever call to inquire about her condition.

When we headed back to Maine in late August of 1983, we stopped in Denver to see Mom and found her greatly improved, although she still needed to use a wheelchair. We said good-bye wondering if we would ever see her again.

CHAPTER TWENTY-SEVEN

Before we left Colorado, Wells and I had decided that the time had at last come to take action to replace Diane as conservatrix. We consulted with Don Taylor, our Estes Park lawyer, who agreed that Diane's general pattern of incompetence warranted a change. He also believed she was violating the "prudent man rule" by refusing ever to sell gold or silver when the price seemed highly advantageous. Although gold-bugs might argue that keeping one's money almost exclusively in gold and silver is eminently prudent, most probate judges would be likely to disagree. That fall Mr. Taylor found us an excellent Denver lawyer named Sterling Ambler, who agreed to handle our case.

Shortly after we arrived back in Maine, we began to get disquieting phone calls from Jack Harrington. He said Diane wanted to pay off the entire debt from Dad to Mom, using both gold and silver, and then have Mom give all the silver to us children. I exploded at that suggestion, saying that we couldn't pay off all the debt at this point without incurring a huge capital gains tax. If we had transferred the silver bars from Dad to Mom when we received them in July before the price rose significantly in the next couple of months, we would have had no tax obligation on that amount, but Diane had not acted quickly enough, as usual. In the last few weeks, we had realized a $25,000 profit on the silver. To transfer it now would mean paying around $10,000 in income tax. Moreover, the entire debt could not be paid unless we put another $120,000 in gold with these bars, thus incurring an additional tax of $21,000.

I argued with Jack that it was absurd to pay over $30,000 in taxes simply to change the name on a pile of gold and silver sitting in the bank vault, when the debt could be paid tax-free at Dad's death. His response was, "Well, the debt has to be paid."

Since the real motive for the debt payment seemed to be to enable Mom to give the silver bars to us children, I told Jack I had decided it was not advisable anyway for her to give away all this silver. Her future financial needs were too unpredictable because she had already exhausted the number of days that Medicare would pay for mental hospitalization. It would be ironic if she gave away a fortune in silver and ended her days in a state mental institution.

A week or two later Jack came up with yet another plan. He wanted Diane to ask the probate judge for permission to give out $200,000 worth of metals from Dad's estate to his heirs, a plan that was once again disastrous from a tax perspective.

In one of his many calls, Jack also said that part of the grand plan was for him to go out to Fairview Terrace and explain to Mom why she should give us children all the silver that she would receive if the debt were paid. The idea was appalling. Since she was in the nursing-home wing recovering from a near fatal illness, she was clearly in no shape to discuss these complex tax issues with such a fast talker. I at once called Diane to say I did not think a high-pressure salesman like Jack should be turned loose on Mom to persuade her to make moves that would only lose us a lot of money and generate a huge profit for him.

All these wild ideas would have alarmed me even more had I not known that Dad had just requested that I replace Diane as conservatrix. Because he was in a less intransigent mood than usual that fall, I had asked him if he had ever considered requesting a change of conservatrix. He replied that he would indeed like someone other than Diane in charge. Dad had never had any respect for her ability as a business-woman. Since she had been conservatrix, he had been constantly upset because she would not discuss any of the estate business with him. He had recently summed up his discontent by saying, "The trouble with Diane is, she thinks my money is her money."

I suggested that either Bob Krotter or I would be a logical replace-ment. Reminding Dad that he had chosen his cousin Bob to be the executor of his will, I told him I would be happy to have Bob serve. A few days later Dad visited his lawyer and signed a paper requesting that I replace Diane in the post of conservatrix. His doctor wrote an accom-panying statement saying he considered Dad sufficiently competent to make that decision. I was now in a strong position to dislodge Diane because the probate judge would give considerable weight to Dad's preference.

In early September, I also talked with Dad's cousin Gene Schroeder, who looked after all our business interests in southwest Nebraska. I explained that I wanted to unseat Diane as conservatrix and asked his opinion on the subject. He offered it freely and in very strong terms. Having dealt with Diane on many estate matters, he recognized her obvious limitations. We both knew that Diane had not been the one who initiated the sale of two of the lumberyards and other Nebraska real estate. Either Gene or I had always started the process and decided what should be done. Sooner or later we talked things over with Diane, and she was the one with the power to make the decisions and sign the papers, but action almost never originated with her. Gene Schroeder and the Nebraska lawyers and accountants had frequently complained that when they sent important papers to her to be signed at once, she was often slow in complying. When they called to ask why they had not received the signed papers, she would say she had not opened her mail for a few days. Two months earlier Diane had received the insurance bill on our Estes Park property and ignored it, so the insurance had lapsed for a few weeks.

Gene agreed a change was desirable and seemed in effect to be saying, "I'm surprised it took you so long to come to this decision." He agreed to talk to Raymond Hanson, who was probably unaware of what had transpired behind the scenes in the Nebraska business transactions while Diane was in charge. I finished the conversation feeling encouraged to proceed.

That Saturday I called Raymond to let him know that Dad's letter requesting that I be conservatrix was on its way to him. Dad's lawyer had directed the letter to Raymond instead of the probate judge. This was unfortunate since he never passed it along to the judge. Raymond was most unpleasant and insisted I had no grounds for seeking to replace Diane. I pointed out that he was not aware of how Diane had handled the bulk of the Nebraska business because he was not directly involved. He did not want to listen to any of this, however, and kept shifting the argument to personal grounds, saying that my action would be very destructive to Mom and Dad. I replied that if Diane were simply to resign as Dad had requested, there would be no battle, so she would also bear responsibility for any ill effects upon Dad or Mom. Raymond then stated that I should just be patient because Diane was planning to distribute some of the metals to the heirs. I insisted that the huge tax bill involved and Mom's poor mental health made these moves very ill-advised.

When Gene Schroeder called Raymond to comment on Diane's management of the Nebraska business affairs, Raymond was unreceptive to the point of rudeness. It was probably naive of me to think that Raymond as the estate lawyer was representing Dad's interests and the principle of justice for all concerned. His loyalties clearly lay with his client Diane.

When I called Diane the next day to inform her of Dad's decision, she had already heard the news from Raymond. Dad's choice clearly angered her because she felt such an overwhelming desire to remain conservatrix to prevent any of the gold and silver being sold. She refused to resign and told me she had been trying to transfer part of the metals to the heirs. Once again I said we would lose money on such a move unless the metal prices doubled before Dad died, a most unlikely scenario. And I also stated once again that Mom's latest mental collapse had convinced me that she should keep most of her money in case she ever needed permanent care in a mental institution. It seemed unthinkable to me that Diane would take any major action to distribute the gold and silver at this point, but I was wrong.

CHAPTER TWENTY-EIGHT

After what I had assumed was a lull in the conservatorship controversy, I received a dismaying phone call from Jack Harrington on Friday evening, October 22, 1982. He said that he had just been to Denver and that Diane had paid off the entire debt of $253,000 from Dad to Mom. He reported that she had used the silver bars, now worth $164,000, and had made up the balance with Canadian Maple Leafs.

"But there weren't any Maple Leafs in the collection," I exclaimed.

"Well," he said, "we traded the brilliant uncirculated $20 gold pieces for the Maple Leafs."

"But that's not a like-kind exchange, Jack," I said. "We would have to pay a capital gains tax on that exchange."

"That's true," he said, "but it doesn't make any difference because we incur the capital gains tax no matter what we use to pay the debt."

"Of course," I said, "that's why I've been saying we shouldn't pay off the debt at this point."

I reminded Jack that I had opposed the idea of trading our brilliant uncirculated $20 gold pieces for more common gold coins when he first suggested it that past summer. The exchange had little to offer to us, but it enriched Jack with a whopping commission of $10,500.

I was so angry I was almost shouting at him over the phone. My mind was racing while we were talking. How could they do this when Diane knew her position as conservatrix was being challenged? To make matters worse, Jack next told me that they had had Mom give away the entire $164,000 worth of silver bars she had just received in payment of the debt.

The worst was yet to come. Jack said they had mailed me my forty-one silver bars. At that news I really exploded. How dared they send me 250 pounds of silver to my local post office without obtaining my permission! I was so furious I could hardly speak. When I demanded why they had not called me to ask what I wanted done with the silver, Jack gave the weak excuse that they had been in a hurry to get everything in the mail and had not had time. It was obvious they had wanted to carry out their elaborate plan before I could stop them.

"You're endangering the security of my family, Jack," I cried. "How could you do this to me? What are people going to think when all that silver arrives at the post office?"

"Oh, you don't have to worry about that," was his glib reply. "I marked the shipment 'machine parts.'"

"Who the hell do you think is going to believe that, Jack? The shipping value of forty grand will be marked right on it," I retorted.

After the conversation with Jack ended, I ran to tell Wells that we were about to receive a shipment of 250 pounds of silver. A gift of that value would normally be a cause for rejoicing, but in this case it was an outright disaster. What in the world were we going to do when the post office notified us of the arrival of the shipment? What could we do with that much silver? Even if the local bank had a vault that large available to rent, it would be impossible to move the silver from the post office to the bank without far too many people being aware of the highly unusual operation. For all we knew, some of the postal employees might think we were keeping the silver bars at home. If word got around town, we could be robbed or threatened.

Wells and I were furious at Diane for visiting this catastrophe upon us. In the face of this latest disaster, we both felt as impotent as we had years before when Diane let Mom descend upon us stark raving mad the night before the auction. I was mortified that Wells was continually forced to cope with these crises that my eccentric family had such a genius for generating. Previously, we had been able to deal with these problems in a relatively private way in Nebraska or Colorado, half a continent away. Now Diane had now dumped a horrendous problem right on our doorstep in Maine.

Wells said immediately that we were not going to accept the silver—our only protection was to say that there had been some mistake and that it should be returned to the sender. I worried, however, that if we let the silver go back to Mom, we might have problems claiming it belonged to us. I didn't approve of Mom giving away that much money, but I didn't want to throw away my share if it were a fait accompli. If I let the post office ship the silver back to Mom and she were to die or slip further into a mentally incompetent state before we arranged to receive the gift in a more convenient way, the silver might legally belong to her and I would be out $40,000.

During the next couple of hours, we discussed the whole episode in a state of extreme agitation. We were sick to think that Diane had needlessly paid off the entire debt, thereby incurring a capital gains tax of more than $40,000. A deposition that my lawyer conducted with Mom a couple of months later contains this highly relevant passage: "Question: 'Did you ever demand payment in full?' Answer: 'Oh, heavens no. I said I couldn't care less. I had more than I could use. It was only a nuisance.'" It also seemed just unbelievable that Jack, Diane, and Raymond had persuaded Mom to give away $164,000 while she was convalescing from an almost fatal illness and her mental state was highly dubious. She was still sleeping at night in the nursing home at the time they had her sign the papers. Their behavior was difficult to understand, particularly when they knew that I was against the transaction and that Mom would not have wanted to go ahead had she known of my opposition. They led her to believe she was doing something very generous for all of us, when she was actually losing us a large sum of money.

It was also incomprehensible that Diane and Raymond had carried out this operation without court sanction when they knew Dad and I were trying to remove her as conservatrix. What seemed particularly flagrant in this case was that the bulk of the money rested in Mom's hands only a few minutes between the time she signed a paper acknowledging receipt of the gold and silver and the time she signed the papers giving the silver away. Diane had acted in such a way as to obtain $40,000 in silver for herself, albeit she received no more than her siblings. It was clearly the kind of maneuver any prudent person would want to perform only with the sanction of the court, especially since the debt existed only through bookkeeping entries.

But what I found hardest to understand was why Diane had rushed ahead with these transactions before the tax issues I had raised were resolved. These transactions had enormous financial implications for all of us, and I had emphatically expressed my opposition to the scheme of having Jack Harrington go out to Fairview Terrace to persuade Mom to do all these things. For Diane to carry out these actions surreptitiously, after I had expressed my strong opposition and had said they would lose us large sums of money, was not only unfair, it was unethical.

But we couldn't turn back the clock. The silver was on its way to our post office, and we couldn't stop it. The next morning I called Sterling Ambler, the Denver estate layer who had just agreed to take my case against Diane. When I told him about the silver shipment, he could see at once why we had a problem with Diane. Sterling and I decided the silver shipment should be returned to him in Denver, where he would store it in a safe deposit box for me.

The next day I received a call from my local post office saying that an insured shipment had just arrived for me. I immediately went down to see about the silver bars. Trying to attract as little attention as possible, I told a clerk that an insured shipment had been sent to me by mistake. When I said I had come down to arrange to return the shipment to Denver, he said he would get the postmaster.

The postmaster walked out of his office, looked at me curiously, and said, "What did you do, rob a silver mine?" This joking remark, made within earshot of a dozen employees and customers, upset me to the point of tears. I feared my family would be endangered if word spread around town that we had received 250 pounds of silver in the mail. Barely able to control my voice, I asked the postmaster in a low tone to be very careful what he said because I was worried about the safety of my family. When he saw how much his flippant remark had disturbed me, he was very apologetic and invited me to come into his office to make arrangements privately.

After I explained that the shipment had been sent to me by mistake, we went out to a security storage area to put new shipping labels on the bags. We also had to put some of the silver into new bags because the canvas on the original ones had torn, exposing the corners of some of the silver bars. Since the shipment carried a value of $40,000 and the heavy objects were clearly rectangular, it couldn't have been more obvious that the bags contained silver bars, even had the canvas not torn. Why Jack had bothered to label the bags "machine parts" was beyond me. Any fool could guess what they contained.

While we were labeling the bags and talking, the postmaster said to me, "Let's see now, your husband teaches at the college, doesn't he?" A woman came by and said with evident curiosity, "Oh, you're the lady I talked to on the phone." Another employee walked by, looked at the pile of bags, and said, "What's all this, Wells Fargo?" He obviously knew what was in the bags. These curious remarks only heightened my concern that there would be talk about the episode that could embarrass or endanger us.

CHAPTER TWENTY-NINE

The next week I flew to Denver, where my new lawyer, Sterling Ambler, and I spent a couple of days discussing my case, which he considered to be unusually complex. He did believe I would be in a strong position to take legal action because the probate code gives the judge the power to set aside any transaction in which the conservator has a substantial conflict of interest. Since Diane had precipitously paid the entire debt, without a real request from Mom, and then immediately persuaded Mom to give most of the money away, with Diane herself receiving $40,000, it seemed obvious she had a conflict of interest. Payment of the debt had cost Dad's estate a huge capital gains tax, as well as a commission of $10,500 for Jack Harrington, so it was clearly not in Dad's interest to pay the debt.

Sterling also thought that the probate judge would honor Dad's request to have me replace Diane as conservatrix. Her lack of competence to manage the estate would be evident from the way she had refused to sell gold and silver when the prices had risen sharply in 1980. After all, Jack Harrington had written a letter stating that the collection had fallen from a peak value of $2,500,000 in January of 1980 to a value of $700,000 in August of 1982.

Another topic Sterling and I discussed was the exchange of the brilliant uncirculated (B.U.) $20 gold pieces for the Canadian Maple Leafs. While I was in Denver, I called Charles Stack, the New York coin dealer who had looked at the hoard, to ask his opinion. He was aghast at the move and said, "Your sister has sold off the cream of the collection." The B.U.'s were indeed the only real numismatic coins we had left. The Maple Leafs would move right down with falling bullion prices, while the B.U.'s would fall only slightly, thus giving us important downside protection. It was incredible to think we had incurred a tax of $20,000 and given Jack a commission of $10,500 in order to trade our B.U. gold pieces for less desirable coins.

Sterling and I were both amused and outraged by the two letters that I had received from Jack Harrington that were to serve as tax documents to accompany the gift from Mom. One ended, "I hope that some day these silver bricks will help build the foundation of your future happiness." The other contained this language: "I wish to transfer these bars to each of you children because they are just too heavy for me to carry around in my purse! . . . I hope that some day this gift will bring you much happiness and fond memories." One thing was obvious–my mother would never have expressed herself in that ridiculous fashion. She didn't write those letters, and I'm sure that neither Diane nor her lawyer wrote them. The irony of the comments is painful, given that the transfer of the silver bars led to the legal battle that embittered Diane against me, with far-reaching consequences. Needless to say, I do not have "fond memories" of the day I received forty-one silver bars at my local post office.

Another troublesome issue that Sterling and I discussed was Mom's competency to give away $164,000. We realized that we would have to tread a very fine line to make the judge clearly aware of Mom's history of frequently recurring mental problems, as well as her recent very poor mental condition, without hurting her by charging publicly that she was incompetent.

Sterling called Raymond to relate my concern about the tax implications of the transactions. Raymond as usual said, "I'm not a tax lawyer, but we have an opinion from our tax lawyer showing the advantages of this course." When Sterling asked if we could see the opinion, Raymond refused to show it to us. The next day we asked if they would bring their tax lawyer to discuss the tax issues with us, but they again refused. This I found very frustrating. These were not emotional questions but basic mathematical tax issues that intelligent and knowledgeable people could look at objectively. If these transactions were not set aside, there were certain tax consequences. We had a short-term gain of $57,000 on the silver bars since July, so we had incurred a tax of over $30,000 by waiting until now to transfer the bars from Dad to Mom. If the judge set aside the debt payment, this tax would be saved.

Before going to Denver, I had called Mom to discuss the transactions with her, saying that I was very upset about the huge tax bill incurred. She said she had been told there would be no tax consequences to the transactions, and she too was very concerned that we would have to pay so much in taxes. When I suggested we might be able to reverse the process, she was eager to do so if it would save the family a large sum of money. It was most unfortunate that she was involved in the whole upsetting business just as she was recovering from her severe illness, but it seemed impossible to insulate her from the battle.

Before I left, Sterling made it clear that he thought we had a strong case and that the chances were good that the judge would set aside the transactions. But he did warn me of the financial risks involved. His time was costing me $100 an hour, and I had already run up an $1,800 bill. It was likely, however, that the judge would assess my costs against the estate if he concluded my action was beneficial to the estate. On the other hand, I could be asked to pay the costs for both sides if my case was judged to be "frivolous" in the legal sense, and that was an unsettling possibility, albeit a remote one.

Wells and I considered carefully the risks and possible gains involved in pursuing legal action. We were more concerned than ever about Diane's judgment and particularly worried about the dangerous influence Jack Harrington had over her. On one occasion that fall when we had been discussing some of the issues, he had said to me, "Don't worry, I'll be able to talk Diane into that." Jack was a very clever person and had figured out just how to handle Diane, playing upon her loneliness. He had established a very friendly personal relationship with her, taking her out to eat and spending long periods talking to her on the telephone. We could envision him continuing to churn commissions by various activities involving the collection, claiming a fee of eight percent of the value of each transaction, a rate other coin dealers later told us was much too high.

On balance, Wells and I decided we had to go ahead with legal action. We had confidence in Sterling Ambler's competence to handle our case, and we believed Diane's actions on October 18 were so flagrant that the judge would be appalled. It also seemed very likely that he would be highly critical of Diane for having held 90 percent of the estate assets in gold and silver without ever availing herself of extremely attractive selling opportunities. Hence I instructed Sterling to proceed with the case, and a hearing date was set for December.

As the middle of November approached, I thought it was essential to get Raymond and Diane to sit down and discuss the tax issues with us. I was very frustrated that she refused to talk to me on the telephone about anything and insisted instead that we pass messages through our lawyers. This was running up legal bills at a fast rate. For me to pass a message to Diane and get a reply meant five expensive steps, each involving one or two lawyers.

I decided it would be cheaper and more efficient for me to return to Denver for a couple of days so that I could talk to Diane directly in the presence of Sterling and Raymond. Accordingly, I flew out on November 18 for a meeting. We had urged Raymond and Diane to bring along their tax lawyer to discuss the tax issues. Once again they refused to do this. We were beginning to doubt whether their tax lawyer approved of their actions since they were so unwilling to produce him. The preceding summer he had told me he didn't think it was worth paying the capital gains tax to pay the debt. At a later date, we discovered that their tax opinion had been written not by their tax lawyer but by one of his young assistants.

Raymond and Diane arrived for the meeting that afternoon in an obviously defensive mood. After a few preliminaries, Sterling again suggested that we would like to have the transactions set aside by the judge on the grounds that Diane had a conflict of interest in the situation. Raymond turned to Diane and burst out angrily, "We don't have to listen to this kind of thing. Should we just leave right now?" They almost walked out, but Sterling managed to calm the situation and they stayed. For the next forty minutes, however, Raymond sat on the edge of his chair, ready to take offense and leave at any moment. After the meeting, Sterling commented that Raymond reminded him of a cornered animal and said that he thought his extremely defensive behavior was an indication of his awareness of his own vulnerability. He had suggested that Mom give away $164,000, with $40,000 going to his client Diane, and Mom had not even had the benefit of independent legal counsel. This was especially egregious given her longstanding mental problems. To make matters worse, as Raymond later testified, he had done this knowing full well he was asking Mom to take an action to which I was opposed.

When we stated our conclusions about the tax consequences of their transaction scheme, Raymond simply once more threw up his hands and said, "I'm not a tax lawyer." The phrase was becoming a knee-jerk response. It was particularly frustrating because they had refused to bring their tax lawyer along. They announced their departure after only an hour, saying Diane had lessons to teach. Since I had flown all the way from New England to talk with them, I was really upset to find out that they had not scheduled a larger block of time for our meeting.

As they were leaving the room, Raymond stopped and said to me, "It is very unfortunate that you would take this action and alienate Diane from her nieces." I viewed that as a veiled threat and fired right back, "I assumed when I started this action that Diane would never leave any of her property to my children anyway. I've already given up on that." While I was in Denver, I invited Dad to come out on the train so he could spend the night with me because he always enjoyed visiting the city. That evening Dad and I ate at a Polynesian restaurant, where the opulent Asian decor fascinated him. Since his heart attack, Dad had developed a childlike appreciation of things about him, and this kind of occasion gave him great pleasure. Before his attack, he had traveled frequently on business trips around Nebraska and Colorado, and he missed eating in good restaurants now that he rarely left Palisade. As we entered the restaurant, Dad saw a display case containing biographies of the founder of the chain. Biography had always fascinated him, so he bought one and enjoyed reading me passages during the rest of his visit. We ate a very leisurely meal, having no other plans for the evening. Dad was delighted that he could order hot buttered rum, served up from a huge cauldron in a quaint sort of goblin mug. It was a happy evening, one that I'll always remember.

The next morning I went to a florist shop, as I felt that despite the present quarrel, I wanted to do something for Diane's birthday the next day. I debated sending her something, not knowing what her attitude would be, but decided to go ahead. I picked out a large plant and arranged to have it delivered to her. After Mom visited Diane the following weekend, I asked her if Diane had received it. She reported that Diane had been so angry she had taken a bus all the way downtown to return the plant to the florist.

Soon after my return home, Sterling called to say that Diane and Raymond were asking for a postponement of the December hearing. Diane was looking for another lawyer to represent her because Raymond was in semiretirement and did not wish to handle the case.

The judge granted their request for a delay, which created a major problem for us. Mom was in a sufficiently good mental state now to testify about her part in the operation, and it was crucial that the judge know she had not really demanded payment of the debt. It was then highly likely he would rule Diane had a conflict of interest. But if Mom slipped mentally and was unable to testify, then the judge could say that the old signed claim form justified Diane's actions.

Since Mom usually experienced a post-Christmas slump, Sterling decided we should take a deposition as soon as possible so that we could fall back on that testimony if she was unavailable for the actual hearing. We were sorry to subject Mom to the strain of a deposition, but it seemed unavoidable, so we scheduled a deposition for early January. I tried to minimize the strain for Mom by explaining that the deposition would be taken quietly in Sterling's office, with only Sterling and Raymond present. I assured her that Sterling was a kind person and would not ask intimidating questions. Although she wasn't happy about it, she seemed to realize that it was unavoidable.

CHAPTER THIRTY

At the end of December, gold and silver prices were substantially up once again, with gold almost $500 an ounce and silver $13 an ounce. We suggested that Diane sell part of the collection at these attractive prices, but Raymond said they would take no action under fire. Unfortunately, that principle hadn't prevented them from implementing the disastrous October 18 manipulations. As it turned out, within the next two years gold dropped to $300 an ounce and silver to $6 an ounce, so we had missed yet another excellent selling opportunity.

Gold and silver problems and a family crisis once again had to be dealt with simultaneously. During my conversations with Jack about a possible compromise, I learned some dismaying news about Kent. When Kent had visited Mom in August, he had told me that he had put his house on the market. I was relieved to hear this, as it was much too large and inefficient a house for an unemployed bachelor. Later I heard that he was having trouble getting his price, and in early November he called to ask me to send him money from Mom's account to rent an apartment. I suggested the amount of $400 because he had found an apartment for $200. I thought he could probably get by on the other $200 for food but told him to call me if he could see he wasn't going to make it through the month. From past experience I knew that he would waste any extra money he received. By this point I had an informal understanding with Mom that I would handle these matters from her account without burdening her.

In early December, Jack Harrington told me that he had seen foreclosure notices for Kent's house in the paper. Jack said he thought he should go over to the house and check up on him, and I agreed that would be a good idea. The next day he reported that he had found Kent lying on the kitchen floor half-frozen in a drunken stupor. Since the fuel company had stopped delivery several weeks earlier, the furnace was no longer operating and the house was bitterly cold. The utilities company had shut off the water, but for some reason the electricity was still on, so Kent was sleeping in front of the electric oven. Its small glowing element could do little to heat the large house, however. Jack had taken

Kent over to his store to thaw him out, and he reported that Kent looked as if he hadn't changed his clothes for a long time and he smelled awful. It was a shocking state of degradation for someone who had been voted "most likely to succeed" in his high school graduating class. By contrast, Clark and Helen Brown's only son, Russell, who was a close friend of Kent's in the class below him, had risen to a top position on the staff of Nick Begich, an Alaskan congressman. Tragically, Russell was on the plane that disappeared over Alaska in 1972 with House Speaker Hale Boggs, Nick Begich, Russell, and a pilot onboard.

Kent grew up with more financial advantages than Russell, but that hadn't kept him from ending up with his life a shambles. Jack had learned that the bank holding the mortgage on Kent's house was willing to have Kent simply sign over the deed. That seemed a good solution to the house problem given the difficulty of selling it in its present filthy condition.

The next problem was to get Kent relocated. I asked Jack why Kent was freezing to death in his unheated house when I had sent him $400 to rent an apartment and buy food. Jack said he had seen a dozen cases of beer at the house and thought most of the money had probably gone for liquor. A dozen cases of beer, thirty cases of orange marmalade, the Krotter men bought in quantity, lest the supply run out. Kent had investigated the possibility of moving into a shelter run by the Salvation Army, and Jack had urged him to do so as soon as possible. Kent had agreed to pack up his things, sell his books, stove, and refrigerator, and be ready to leave within a week. When Jack checked back a few days later, however, he found Kent was making no progress whatever but had just settled down to drink. Finally, Jack had to take charge and bring in people to buy Kent's things.

Jack must have had a strong stomach to be able to keep going over to the house. He reported that the overpowering stench almost knocked him down when he opened the front door. When I asked how Kent had managed to live for weeks without running water, Jack told me the sordid details. The kitchen counters and the sink were piled high with dirty dishes because there was no way to wash them. The room reeked with the odor of decaying food scraps. But worst of all, Kent had continued to eliminate in the bathroom, despite the absence of running water. What puzzled me was that the realtor was still showing people through the house right up to the time Kent signed over the deed. Real estate agents may be a glib lot, but I cannot imagine what this one said as he opened the bathroom door. It was indeed ironic that Mom and Grandmother Krotter had foregone the new houses they had wanted so much in order to save the money that eventually paid for this house.

Each day Jack called me with a report. Soon I dreaded to pick up the phone and hear the latest. Now that Kent had signed the deed, it was essential to get him out of the house. Jack called me late on the day the final exit was to have taken place. He reported that Kent had been very upset at the low price a book dealer had given him for his books and had gone out the door carrying a small tool box. I shuddered when I heard that and told Jack that when Diane and I had closed out Kent's apartment when he left Denver years ago, we had found a revolver in a tool box.

Early that evening Jack went back over to the house to see if Kent had returned. Kent was nowhere to be seen, but Jack could hear his cat meowing in the attic, which was accessible by a stairway. Jack and I had agreed he shouldn't deal with Kent in the final eviction without someone along for protection, so he got a friend to join him before investigating the attic. Caution was all the more important now that we knew Kent was carrying around a gun. They discovered Kent shivering in the attic, surrounded by boxes of the emergency rations that people of the doomsday persuasion stockpile so they will have something to eat when the government collapses. It seemed a bitterly ironic commentary upon my father's philosophy, which had been so completely adopted by Kent and Diane. Kent's personal doomsday was much more imminent than the bankruptcy of America.

As soon as Jack entered the attic, he noticed a revolver lying on the floor a few feet from Kent. Two possibilities quickly crossed his mind. Was Kent contemplating suicide or was he perhaps going to shoot anyone who tried to evict him from the house? Neither Kent nor Jack alluded to the presence of the gun, and Jack hastily thought of a plan to get rid of it. He said, "Well, Kent, we had better load out all these boxes of rations, hadn't we?" Kent agreed, so Jack and his friend began to move everything out. Jack put a stack of boxes down on top of the gun and then picked up the gun with the boxes and carried it out. Kent never mentioned the disappearance of the gun. After the boxes were all removed, Jack said to Kent, "Hadn't you better go on over and check into the shelter for the night? You'll freeze to death if you stay here." Kent agreed to go over soon. That was the point at which Jack called me to relate what was going on. Jack said he was worried he might find

Kent dead the next morning, but he didn't see what he could do about the situation. I myself saw no alternative because we could not force Kent to go over to the shelter.

The next day Jack called to report that he had found the house empty when he checked on Kent that morning. He then went over to the Salvation Army shelter to find out if Kent had gone there. At first they were reluctant to give Jack any information, but finally someone told him that Kent was in the city hospital. As it turned out, he had attempted to assemble a second gun to shoot himself. When he couldn't get the gun put together, he gave up and called a former counselor to tell him he had attempted suicide. The counselor was the one who arranged to have Kent admitted to the city hospital.

All this appalling turmoil in Kent's life occurred only a week before Christmas, which made it particularly upsetting for me to deal with the crisis. When our own house was filled with warmth, good food, and all the pleasures of Christmas, it was especially depressing to think of Kent living in filth and squalor in an icy cold house. At least it was a relief to know that he was at last out of the house and into a hospital.

Jack reported that he had gone over to the hospital to talk to Kent, who was still very depressed and insisted he wanted to die. Jack promised to keep track of the situation for the family. It was really awkward to use him to do these things, but I saw no good alternative. After several days, Jack let me know that Kent had been discharged from the hospital and had gone to the Salvation Army center for alcoholics.

The general policy of the center was to dry people out for thirty days and then to place them in jobs. As Kent was always a difficult case to reassimilate into society, a year later he was still living in the Salvation Army. I made an occasional call to the general of the Salvation Army, who told me Kent was proving very useful to them working in their office. He said to me, "You would be proud of him." Although that didn't quite sum up my feelings about Kent, I was happy to know he was functioning again.

It was strange to think that Kent was living in the Salvation Army, when his family had a small fortune in gold and silver, but it was probably the situation most conducive to his welfare. The Salvation Army at least stopped him from drinking and did something to rehabilitate him. If he had had family money supporting him, he would have holed up in a house or apartment, drinking his life away and never doing a day's work.

CHAPTER THIRTY-ONE

Sterling Ambler took Mom's deposition on January 4. Her testimony clearly helped our case because she was obviously very confused about the whole October operation. For example, she testified that she had given only one bar of silver to her brother and one to her sister, while in fact she had given Uncle Max four bars and Aunt Thelma five bars. After he read the document, Dad's lawyer commented, "What I can't figure out is why your mother hasn't been declared incompetent." (She had in fact been declared incompetent at one point, but the ruling was lifted when she had a prolonged good period.)

Mom's testimony included the following passages:

Question: All right, Mrs. Krotter, the claim says "plus interest until paid." What rate of interest were you thinking of in that respect?

Answer: Well, whatever was the going rate of interest. Some of it was pretty good. I wouldn't charge my husband interest for his part of the estate. But whoever wanted a piece of it, if they were real anxious, could have it, but they would have to pay interest until it was paid up. . . .

Question: Now at the early part of 1982 Dean had filed a petition to terminate the conservatorship, hadn't he? Do you recall that? . . .

Answer: There was none filed, and it was my daughter Alison if it was, which I happen to know, and they dropped it. Dean might have thought about it. I don't live with my husband, you know. We are very friendly.

Question: Did you ever demand payment in full?

Answer: Oh, heavens no. I said I couldn't care less. I had more than I could use. It was only a nuisance. . . .

Question: Now I hand you what's been marked Petitioner's Exhibit B [the claim form] and ask you if you can identify that.

Answer: $220,000 in principal and $33,000 in interest, yes, and I accepted that payment, but it was in Engelhard silver at 9.78 an ounce, making the estate $250,000, half a million. Oh, boy, what do you do with half of a million?   . . .

Question: Didn't you tell Alison that you wouldn't have taken the payment if it would cause income tax liability to Dean?

Answer: Yes. . . . Well, I trusted them to get the income tax, whatever it was, straight. I believed they could do a better job than I could on how much was this going to cost Mr. Krotter's estate. It wouldn't have made any difference to me. It might have to Alison. Briefly, because I wasn't allowed to digest some of this. But it didn't make any difference. But I was quite sure Diane had gone through it and was right, and it wouldn't make any difference about the–Anyway, in either case, if I had it to do again I would–if I knew it was going to affect Dean's, I couldn't have cared less, because he doesn't need it and I don't need it.

Question: Okay, let's talk about the gifts to your children a bit now. On October 18, 1982, at or about the same time the payment was made to you, you also made some gifts to your children, didn't you; is that correct?

Answer: No.

Question: You did not make any gifts to your children in October 1982?

Answer: No. We talked about it, but I decided not until this was settled.

Question: So you still have the—

Answer: Now wait a minute. Let me think. Maybe $125,000–in October? 1982?

Question: Just last year.

Answer: Just let me think. I remember the two silver bars. Yes, but I don't know that there were any–We talked about it and what it would be. Yes, I guess it was indicated. I didn't think I carried out some of that, though. They told me that I would write checks to my four children. That was right. I did, I gave the four children straight, I gave them a gift of 253–the $253,000.

Question: You gave gifts to the children—

Answer: Not all of that certainly.

Question: —to the four? Do you recall about how much you gave to each child?

Answer: About two hundred—

Question: No, to each of the four children.

Answer: I know. Divide–I was supposed to keep half of it in my own account. The other–that would be $125,000, a quarter of a million, because I remember it went to the children, was to go to the children, all of them equal. . . . I don't remember exactly what that came to, but it was–I got it down someplace, four portions of a half of $253,000 . . .

Question: Mark's share did not go to Canada then?

Answer: No, I don't think so.

Question: It's still here in Denver—

Answer: I don't know. I think it's part of–If he didn't want it, he didn't want it, so you just don't bother about it. It's a good idea, if you are not going to get mixed up with things, why should you get the benefits of what the family wants? So they asked him as a matter of courtesy–he's one of the four children–"We are going to divide this up," and this part he didn't, I don't think, care about. Sometimes, if it was the whole estate, why, of course, he would take it, because, after all, he's–for him–I don't know where it is. He may have dug a hole and put it in Canada in a hole. . . .

Question: Well, maybe I should back off a little bit. Before the debt was paid to you and not counting the fact that Dean owed you more than $200,000, what was the approximate value of your assets?

Answer: Already half a million, and–I mean a quarter of a million, and if they came over, it would be a half a million.

Question: So your assets were worth about a quarter of a million before payment of the debt?

Answer: Yes, I think so. [Her other assets were actually worth no more than $125,000.]

*   *   *   *

The deposition is of course very pathetic. Mom was hopelessly confused by these complex maneuvers and obviously thought she had given away $125,000, when she had actually given away $164,000–$155,000 to her children and $9,000 to her brother and sister. This left her with only $89,000 worth of gold Maple Leafs from the debt payment, whereas she clearly thought she was keeping back half for herself.

When the January hearing was only a couple of weeks away, Diane and Raymond petitioned the court for a continuance because they still did not have a lawyer. The judge granted a postponement to March 30, but in mid-February Diane and Raymond announced that the lawyer whom they had been consulting could not take the case because of health problems. They were now looking for a new lawyer. This was dismaying news, with the hearing only six weeks away. In late February we heard they had engaged a lawyer named Edward Murphy. Since he required more time to prepare for the hearing, they were requesting yet another postponement. Their actions seemed to be a stalling technique.

I was upset to see the case dragging on and on, as though it were a perpetual condition of life. We all needed to achieve a speedy legal resolution so we could get on with our lives. I was also alarmed by the rapidly mounting legal costs. In his initial letter to me, Sterling Ambler had said that his fees incurred on my behalf could run as high as $20,000 or $30,000. With the hearing date moved later and later, I was worried about the costs pushing well beyond that range. My legal bills had already exceeded $11,000, and the final preparations and the hearing itself would add significantly to that amount. If we delayed the hearing by weeks or months, far more money would be required.

As it turned out, however, the judge granted their request for postponement, pushing the date all the way back to June 21.

CHAPTER THIRTY-TWO

At the end of May, both sides met at the Denver Probate Court for a hearing on a motion filed by Gerald Smith, Dad's Nebraska lawyer, asking that regular quarterly payments of $2,500 be made to Dad so that he could have some money to invest. The hearing turned out to be a useful dry run for the trial because it gave us some feeling for the judge's opinion on the case. He made it clear early in the session that he was shocked that an estate of this size was all tied up in gold and silver and had virtually no income-producing property. After perhaps fifteen minutes spent in a formal hearing, the judge suggested we all recess to his chambers for an informal discussion of the issues. During that time he remarked that he had once known someone like this who was saving up gold and silver against some future Armageddon. When he commented that we might be dealing with a bit of a miser instinct here, Sterling and I could hardly suppress our amusement. Little did he know that we had not one but two misers in this case.

We were pleased with these indications that the judge was not at all sympathetic to the gold-bug point of view. On the other hand, we were dismayed to find out that he wanted Dad to appear in court to state in person that he preferred me as conservatrix, instead of simply relying on his letter. This of course raised great problems. Only six weeks earlier Dad had again been hospitalized for heart irregularities, so we were very reluctant to submit him to the stress of cross-examination.

While Sterling and I were discussing this point, he mentioned that it would also be necessary to call Mom as a witness. I found this very upsetting because I had assumed that her deposition would suffice. Sterling said, however, that customarily you use a deposition in lieu of live testimony only if the person is unable to appear and that we would at least need agreement from the other side to accept the deposition in lieu of live testimony. Even then the judge might be reluctant to settle for the deposition when Mom lived right in Denver. I certainly didn't like the idea of bringing Mom into the actual hearing.

On the other hand, it was crucial for us to establish the fact that she had not really asked for payment of the debt by Dad but had had it instead thrust upon her by Raymond and Diane. During the next few days, we pondered these problems while moving ahead in the preparation of the case, which was scheduled to go to pretrial in less than two weeks. Everyone was now feeling the pressure of the impending trial. In the course of one of our conversations, a Colorado lawyer who was assisting Gerald Smith proposed we settle the issue by dividing up Dad's estate into two halves for Diane and me to administer. This seemed like a viable option because I wouldn't necessarily want to sell more than half of Dad's hoard at this point anyway. Since Diane had repeatedly said no to dividing up the pile in the past, however, I wasn't optimistic that she would be any more receptive to the idea now.

The legal costs were mounting to frightening levels. I had already incurred $32,000 in legal fees, and the fees for Diane's new lawyer, Ed Murphy, were probably not much less. If the battle continued through a three-day trial as planned, it was conceivable that the fees could end up in the neighborhood of $50,000 for each side. The financial risk involved if we lost was becoming unacceptable. I was still convinced of the merits of the case and thought it very likely that we would win. But even if the judge ruled against Diane, he might think that she was just very misguided and not assess the costs of the case to her. If the estate ended up paying all the legal fees, this would further reduce my eventual inheritance.

The other great drawback to proceeding to trial was, of course, the fact that both Dad and Mom would have to be called as witnesses in order for us to make a strong case. I hated to expose them to that much trauma. Sterling was also personally reluctant to take this step. A few weeks earlier he had said to me, "This case is eating out my insides."

All things considered, Sterling and I decided this proposal of dividing the metals was worth discussing, so we made an exploratory call to Ed Murphy. He expressed interest, perhaps because they were disheartened by the judge's remarks in the informal hearing that indicated little sympathy with their point of view. Probably Diane was also frightened by the soaring legal costs.

Sterling and Ed arranged to meet the following day. At the end of the meeting, Sterling called to say that Ed and Diane were willing to compromise along those lines but insisted that two-thirds of the metals remain with Diane as conservatrix and one-third be administered by me in a trust for Dad. Although I wasn't happy about taking a reduced share, I finally decided to accept the division to reach a compromise. Diane's psychological attachment to the gold and silver was so great that I knew it would be difficult to pry any more of the hoard loose from her grasp.

Diane and I signed an agreement to this effect the following day. Fortunately, the probate judge charged to Dad's estate the fees of $38,000 for Sterling, $30,000 for Ed, and $3,000 for Dad's Nebraska and Colorado lawyers. He remarked in passing that he was pleased that he would not have to read the voluminous materials involved in the case.

I went back to Estes Park with a sense of relief that the long ordeal was over but also with a feeling of immense frustration that it had not been possible to obtain justice. I was still convinced that Diane had grossly mismanaged the estate affairs and lost all of us a huge amount of money, but I didn't want to risk going broke just to prove my point. Even if the judge had assessed the enormous legal fees involved against Diane, it would have been a Pyrrhic victory for me. Of course, I was extremely angry with her, but not to the extent of $100,000. I wanted her removed from office, not financially ruined. The whole case confirmed how difficult it can be to obtain justice in our system if you are not extremely rich. Although we informed the probate court that one of its conservatorships was being grossly mismanaged, we couldn't even get the judge to focus his attention on the merits of the case without spending $50,000.

The year-long battle had left us all exhausted, but I thought we still had an important piece of unfinished business to address. This was the question of Mom's remaining property, which I thought should be put into a trust. It was abundantly clear by now that she was not really competent to handle it. Having seen how Jack and Diane had manipulated her, I worried about what might happen if Kent and his con-man friend decided to approach Mom with some wild financial scheme.

I also strongly urged Mom to replace Raymond Hanson as the trustee of the trust she had established for Kent. By this point, I had no confidence whatever in Raymond's business judgment and feared he might give Kent too much control over his money. After all, he had wanted to give Kent money to start a used trailer business with his con-man friend. My apprehension was only increased when Raymond one day said to me, "That boy's got a good head on his shoulders."

I took Mom to see a Denver lawyer, Bob Ward, who was an old family friend from Palisade whose father had been one of Dad's business partners. Bob himself had worked in Dad's office for a year or so. At any rate, he recommended that her property be put into trust with the trust department of a major bank. Mom, Mr. Ward, and I all agreed that this action would help insulate her from any further disagreements about her estate. Mom was receptive to the idea, and Aunt Thelma, who was visiting us, encouraged the plan. When we first met with Mr. Ward, Diane refused to join us but sent a message through Ed Murphy saying that she would stay out of the whole affair and that Mom could do as she pleased. Unfortunately, after further thought, Diane wrote the following letter to Mr. Ward, sending copies of it to all concerned:

> I am writing this letter to advise you formally of my opposition to the placement of my mother's estate in trust.
> . . .
> I have defended this retention of precious metals in the estates of both my parents . . . because I have deep respect for my father's viewpoint in this matter, and heartily concur in it. Because I know full well that this is, at present, a minority viewpoint (my father used to say that the best kind of minority was a minority of one), I am loath to see the administration of this estate pass into the hands of an unknown quantity in the form of a trustee who may or may not share these views . . .

Of course, Mom was reluctant to proceed after Diane wrote this letter. She did not put her money into a trust, nor did she replace Raymond Hanson as trustee of Kent's trust. Once I saw Diane's letter, I gave up trying to get a rational solution. It was hopeless to deal with Diane, and nothing was going to change that.

My fears that Raymond Hanson would not administer Kent's trust properly were well founded. After moving out of the Salvation Army in 1984, Kent lived in an apartment and worked as a bus person in a fast-food restaurant for several years. In 1991, Raymond Hanson unfortunately paid him the entire balance of his trust, $66,000, confirming my worst fears. By 1994, Kent had lost all this money on bad investments. When his apartment rent was raised substantially, he had to move back to the Salvation Army.

That August it was clear that Diane had no intention of ever resuming a normal relationship. I had invited Aunt Thelma to visit us in July. She told me that Diane had asked her to stay over with her in August but had said, "Don't expect me to participate in any family dinners or picnics." After Diane arrived, she even went to the absurd length of refusing to ride with me when Mom, Aunt Thelma, Diane, and I were invited to social occasions. She insisted on driving separately, which only made Mom feel bad, although Aunt Thelma and I could laugh it off.

I felt sorry for Mom because she was in a low state mentally and physically that August, and it wasn't easy for her to spend time with us. It was a major effort for her to walk up the hill to the upper cabin where my family was spending the month of August. Given Diane's attitude, I did not feel free to go down to the main cabin to join Mom and Aunt Thelma when they were sitting out on the back terrace in the morning. Only when Diane drove off could I go down to the main cabin to spend some time with them.

CHAPTER THIRTY-THREE

At the end of that August of 1983, we again returned to Maine. That fall when I talked to Mom on the telephone, she did not sound at all well. Her doctor said she had developed hives, which he had treated with cortisone. She also had a considerable tremor and was having difficulty walking. The doctor thought this was related to her lithium level because he could eliminate the tremor by withdrawing her lithium. He was attempting to find a proper level of lithium that would keep her on an even-keel emotionally, while preventing the tremor.

In early November, I learned that Mom was not always able to go down to the dining room for meals. I got what information I could from Diane, but it was not easy to talk to her. During one conversation, she slammed down the receiver, saying, "You can go to hell." Diane did tell me she had arranged to have meals brought to Mom on a tray temporarily. The staff of Fairview Terrace had told her, however, that if Mom wasn't able to go to the dining room after a few days, she would have to move into the nursing home wing. When I called the visiting nurse a few days later, she told me Mom had indeed been moved there. This news was particularly upsetting because I knew how much Mom hated the nursing home and how rapidly her condition had deteriorated the last time she went there.

On Friday evening a week after Thanksgiving, the head nurse called to tell me that Mom had taken a sharp turn for the worse. After consulting with Diane, I made arrangements to fly out on Sunday, December 4. That Saturday I called Bonnie Ferguson, Dad's housekeeper, to warn her that it appeared Mom was dying and we might all soon be returning to Palisade for services. She reported that Dad's feet had been swelling because of his poor circulation. Although she didn't think it was anything serious, she intended to take him to see the doctor on Monday. We both agreed she should not mention Mom's illness to him, since he would be very upset by the news.

When I arrived at Fairview, I saw Diane having a cup of coffee in the dining room and joined her. She told me she wasn't sure Mom knew her and said she could no longer talk. In addition, she gave me the disturbing news that Bonnie Ferguson had just called to say that she had sent Dad to the hospital in an ambulance that morning because the swelling in his feet had increased so much that he couldn't walk.

Diane and I went down the hall to Mom's room. She was breathing hard and had a faraway look in her eyes, but when I approached the bed and kissed her, she started trying to move her head and hands. Diane and I were sure she recognized me. I was thankful to have arrived in time for that. Mom was sufficiently aroused that we thought she knew Diane was there also, but she was unable to speak a word. We tried to tell her again how much we loved her and what a wonderful mother she had been to us. After sitting by her bed for a while, we went out to the lobby to talk a minute before Diane left. We both thought Mom was dying, but it was hard to say when she might slip away. Diane decided to teach her students the next day since the situation was unpredictable and I would be there with Mom.

I went up to Mom's apartment to have something to eat and then went back down to her room. This time she barely reacted to my arrival, so I just sat beside her bed and read, holding my hand on her arm, so that she would know I was there if she were sufficiently conscious to be aware of anything. After an hour or so, I happened to glance up and to my horror, saw a mouse in the corner of the room. Mom had always been extremely afraid of mice and I was too, so I put my feet up on the bed right away. I watched, almost frozen in place, while the mouse crawled back into the closet and then came out again. When it retreated once more into the closet, I made some noise to scare it into staying there and quickly left the room, glad Mom wasn't conscious enough to know about the mouse. I went down the hall to the nurse's station to complain, but the nurse on duty just casually remarked that field mice sometimes came in to the building. It horrified me to think of all those little old ladies trapped in their beds and wheelchairs, terrified of mice from which they couldn't escape. At any rate, I wasn't about to have my mother die in a room with a mouse creeping around. So many things had gone wrong in her life, I wanted her to be able to die in peace and dignity at least. Fortunately, when I told the nurse I wanted Mom shifted immediately to another room far away from the mouse, she complied at once.

About 10 o'clock I went up to Mom's apartment to spend the night. Earlier that evening, I had called Bonnie Ferguson to see how Dad was getting along. She reported that when she had visited him that afternoon, he was in good spirits and talked about going home the next day. I asked her to let me know at once if it ever appeared he was dying. If Mom was no longer aware of my presence, I might decide to go out to Nebraska to be with Dad instead. Bonnie replied that there seemed to be no danger at the moment. After making calls to Wells and Aunt Thelma, I went to bed. About 12:40 A.M. I was awakened by the telephone. It was a nurse from the Imperial, Nebraska, hospital calling to say that Dad had died a few minutes before. She had been talking to him earlier and had left the room for a few minutes. By the time she returned, he was dead. I was overwhelmed to think that he had died while we were all expecting Mom to go, and I regretted very much that I wasn't there with him at the end.

That night I slept fitfully, with a mouse crawling in and out of my nightmares. I also dreamed that there had been some mistake and Dad was still alive after all. It was hard to realize he was gone. We had loved each other very much; I was the only one of his children who had maintained a close relationship with him over the years. While his faults were readily apparent to me, I could still appreciate his good qualities and see that he had tried in his own distorted way to be a good father. Dad's whole personality and character somehow were put together a little skewed. We often faulted him for his lack of human sensitivity, but I sometimes felt it was like complaining that a dyslexic child couldn't write his letters in the right direction. Dad just perceived the world from his own special slant. I still found him lovable in spite of it.

The next morning I called Diane and the other relatives with the news. I also talked to our Palisade relatives and to our old friend Helen Brown. She reported to me that Bonnie had told Dad I was in Denver and he had been expecting to see me, talking happily of all the things he wanted to show me. I was so glad to know that in his last hours he had been eagerly looking forward to seeing me.

I spent most of the morning with Mom, who was still only semiconscious. After lunch, I called Diane to let her know that I thought the end might be close, although the nurses would not hazard a guess on how long Mom would last. By now I felt overwrought emotionally. I wanted time to think of Dad and absorb the grief I experienced at his passing. I was caught, however, in a state of extreme emotional tension, hoping the timing would somehow work out so that I could be with Mom when she died and also attend Dad's services in Nebraska.

All that day I sat beside Mom, only making a brief trip up to the apartment to eat lunch. She was breathing in a very labored way, which made me think she could not hold on more than a day or two. The nurses said she was not reacting to stimuli, so they were sure she was not feeling any pain. To pass the time, I sat reading by the bed, with my hand always on her arm, hoping she might be aware that I was there with her. I happened to be rereading Albert Camus's *La Peste*, and his depiction of human response to suffering during a massive outbreak of the plague seemed strangely appropriate. By six o'clock I was beginning to think about going up to the apartment for a bite of soup, but I kept delaying, thinking I would stay a little longer with Mom. One of her friends dropped by to see how she was doing and asked if there was any way she could help. I told her I would like to have a radio so I could play some music to shut out all the unpleasant sounds from the hall. The friend returned at once with her portable radio. I hoped that even in her semiconscious state Mom would be aware of it since she had always loved classical music. The strains of music filling the room seemed to isolate Mom and me on our own little island, blotting out all the distressing noises of the nursing home. The only sounds in the room were the music and Mom's labored breathing, which continued without respite. As seven o'clock came and went, I again considered going upstairs for something to eat, but I decided just to stay with Mom a while longer. A few minutes before 8 o'clock a nurse came in to check her vital signs. When I looked up, I was aware of the sudden absence of that tortured breathing. There was a feeling of quiet peace in the room, and I knew Mom's long ordeal was over. She was free at last.

When I went upstairs to the apartment, I found it hard to believe that Dad and Mom had died the same day, December 5, 1983, neither knowing the other was ill. After they had lived separately for fourteen years, it seemed a remarkable ending to their lives. They still felt close to each other, and it would have been a shock for either to have known the other had died. This way they were spared that grief. The coincidence of their deaths seemed to be a final reunification after the circumstances of their lives had parted them. But it also crossed my mind that even in death, Mom had been unable to escape from her entanglement with Dad. It seemed especially ironic that after years of legal and financial discussion about the consequences of one parent predeceasing the other, they had confounded all speculation by dying on the same day.

Diane and I agreed it would be best to have the services for both Dad and Mom on Thursday. We decided we would have two separate but consecutive services at the church and then go out to the cemetery for graveside services. We were planning to have Dad buried in the Krotter plot, but we knew Mom had wanted to be cremated and have her ashes buried in her parents' plot. I think she had always felt the Krotters were an alien breed and wanted in death to return to her own family. We realized, however, that our decision would afford a final opportunity to the townspeople of Palisade to raise their eyebrows in disbelief.

For a long time that evening, I sat there in Mom's apartment, thinking about her life. She had been a gifted and positive person, whose large capacity for enjoying life had been stunted and cramped by her marriage to Dad. Her own virtues had sealed her fate. Because she was unwilling to hurt my father by leaving him, she stayed with a marriage that could never really work. The uneasiness of their relationship and Dad's unusual character traits together contributed to producing three children who were not happy or well adjusted. I felt fortunate that in the general family shipwreck I had managed to have a happy life.

Mom's last few years were terribly difficult. Aunt Thelma told me Mom would sometimes sit and weep, saying bitterly, "Just look at me, Thelma, Kent's an alcoholic, and I haven't heard from Mark in years, and the girls don't get along." She had invested her whole life in her children, only to find them a source of great worry and concern in her final years.

As I reflected on Mom's life, there came to mind a phrase Aunt Thelma and Mom had often used from their Nebraska Methodist background, saying that in heaven people would have stars in their crowns for every good thing they had done in their life. But Mom didn't really believe in religion, although she went through the motions by habit, and I too no longer believe. So for me Mom's life was cut off once and for all that evening of December 5, with no hope that the scales would ever be balanced for her. For Mom there is no heaven and no starry crown, only the love and admiration of Diane and myself, who before long will be the only people who have any real conception of the kind of person she was and what she endured by sticking with a poor marriage.

While I was sorting through some old papers that summer, I ran across a newspaper clipping announcing that Mom had won an essay contest at the University of Nebraska. As I read her essay, I was struck by its ironic relationship to her life. The assigned topic was "The Rewards and Obligations of the College Student." She began as follows:

An old fable tells the story of a certain rich man, who being desirous of helping someone wished to find one worthy of such help. He finally conceived the idea of moving a huge stone directly in the road which passed by his estate. Beneath the stone, he placed a purse filled with gold as a fitting reward to the one, who with the idea of service to others in mind, would move the stone. He then hid by the roadside to watch the outcome of his philanthropy. Many passed by but each merely turned out of the obstructed roadway and went around the stone. No one seemed willing to assume the obligation of moving the obstacle, thereby helping himself and others who would come after him. Consequently, none received the generous reward. Finally, at dusk, a peasant returning from work, laid down his burden, pushed the cumbersome stone from the road, and was rewarded by the purse of gold. So it is with most life situations. Obligations and rewards are closely linked.

The last sentences were written in a glow of youthful optimism. In retrospect, they are poignantly ironic. Mom spent her life moving huge obstacles with the idea of service to others, but the gold at the end turned out to be a curse instead of a reward.

When Kent came home for the services, we learned that he was now managing a Salvation Army bookstore in Ohio. He was reorganizing it and sorting the books into categories, which gave him a feeling of accomplishment. We were happy to know he was doing something that interested him but regretted that he had not written this news to Mom. She would have been pleased to know he was settled to that extent. Mark did not come to Nebraska but came to Denver a few weeks later for a memorial service for Mom. He told me later that he had been reluctant to come to Palisade because he was afraid there might be unpleasant scenes since he had gone to Canada to avoid the Vietnam War. I doubt if people really cared that much at this point, but I suppose the issue remained ever fresh in his mind. It pleased me that he honored Mom by coming to Denver for the memorial service, but I couldn't forgive him for letting her die without having once heard from him during the last five years. He only acknowledged her existence by endorsing the checks for several thousand dollars which she sent every year as annual exclusion gifts. His cold behavior was a source of constant grief to her, and her joy would have been immeasurable had he just once come to see her during those last years or even just called. What made his attitude even harder to comprehend was that Mom had always been so good to him and had supported him wholeheartedly when he decided to go to Canada. Her only mistake, perhaps, was to have indulged him to excess.

Diane and I went out to Palisade together on Tuesday night. Our first day back in Palisade was very busy with preparations for the services. We had to write out obituaries to be used in the newspaper and also as a guide to the minister, who had moved to Palisade only a few months earlier and did not know much about either Dad or Mom. Things had been going relatively smoothly between Diane and me to that point, but we soon found ourselves in violent disagreement on the obituaries. I was writing up Dad's in reasonably standard form when Diane started insisting we should say that he had been a champion of the gold standard and a backer of the Libertarian Party. Her suggestion was upsetting to me because I thought it was in poor taste to make a political statement through an obituary. Diane was adamant on the subject, however, and I began to wonder how we were going to settle this issue without a nasty fight. When I went to town to get some groceries, I stopped at a pay phone and called Gene Schroeder's wife to see what she thought of the idea. She too was horrified by Diane's proposal. I also checked with Helen Brown, who said, "Oh, you can't mention the word 'gold' in the obituary. People would think you were rubbing their noses in it." I went back to the house fortified with these opinions and stood my ground. As a compromise, I finally suggested that I write Dad's obituary and she write Mom's because I thought there was less potential for problems there.

The whole argument reminded me that eight or ten years earlier Dad had said that at his funeral he wished to have various quotations read from Ayn Rand's philosophical book *Anthem*. Imagine what the townspeople of Palisade would have thought to hear those atheistic and blatantly egocentric statements read out at a funeral in the Methodist Church. Thank goodness Dad either changed his mind or neglected to leave instructions for us to carry out these wishes.

At the services the minister selected a startling text to read for Dad. After puzzling over his choice, I decided he had made it in all innocence as a newcomer to town who knew little about Dad. At any rate, he chose to read the Nineteenth Psalm, which contains the strangely appropriate words:

The judgments of the Lord are true and righteous altogether.
More to be desired are they than gold, yea, than much fine gold.

Epilogue

After a twenty-year hiatus, the eleventh hour came roaring back with a vengeance as the earlier family obsession with gold and silver was replaced by an obsession with the Estes Park land, an obsession that led to a divorce between Wells and me, even though we had had virtually no arguments in forty years of marriage.

One sometimes learns things about the complexity of human relationships that one would rather not have known. It was a very sad point in my life when I realized that my husband and our two older daughters loved my Estes property more than they loved me.

In 2002, the family land holdings in Estes totaled 105 acres and consisted of five lots. My sister Diane, my brother Mark, and I owned the lower four lots, which contained the large log cabin and two smaller cabins. The controversy that led to our divorce revolved around a 45-acre lot up the mountainside that Diane, Mark, Wells, and I had purchased in 1972 from an old family friend and neighbor for the remarkable price of less than $100 an acre. That lot began just above our upper guest cabin and then crossed a steep ravine and ran up a fairly steep mountainside, eventually arriving at some lovely meadows with incredible views of the snow-capped peaks of the Front Range. Perhaps two or three times a year, we would hike up to those meadows for a picnic. Given the steepness of the terrain, it would take us twenty-five minutes or so to reach the meadows.

Even while my parents were still alive, Wells, the girls, and I had frequent conversations about our fears that we might some day lose Estes if Diane left her share outside the family, as she had said she would during a meeting in a lawyer's office and had implied at other times. After the folks died, we also began to wonder if Mark's share of the property might be at risk, given his aloof behavior to the family since his divorce. He had come to Estes only twice since his marriage collapsed, the last occasion being in 1992. Mark's attitude toward Kent when his life was sadly deteriorating was as cold as had been his attitude toward Mom and Dad. When Kent could no longer work as a busboy at a fast-food chain because of his emphysema, I asked Diane and Mark to join me in buying him a combination TV-video player for Christmas so that he would have something to entertain him when he was housebound as an invalid. As I recall, we each needed to contribute about $100. When I talked to Mark, he asked if Kent couldn't get a used set cheaper at the Salvation Army. (At this point, Mark was a leading public prosecutor in Canada, so a $100 gift was hardly beyond his means.)

In January of 2002, when I went out to Ohio to see Kent, who was dying in a nursing home, I telephoned Mark and begged him to call Kent or to send flowers or at least a card. It would have meant so much to Kent, who hadn't heard from Mark in twenty years. My request fell on deaf ears, as had another request years earlier when I begged Mark to at least send Mom a card when she was dying. When Mark died three years later, I was struck by the painful irony of a remark one of his closest friends made to me after his memorial service in Vancouver. "Mark never forgot a birthday or holiday," she said.

From occasional phone conversations with Mark, I knew he wanted no change in the Estes cabins or land. He was dead set against anyone in the family ever building another cabin on the property, which seemed particularly unreasonable because he so rarely came to Estes, and then only for a week's visit.

That's where things stood in the summer of 2002 when Wells and I were making plans to build a retirement house in Brunswick on a beautiful lot in the countryside half a mile from the ocean. As I was designing the house, which we held to about 2,300 square feet, it became apparent that we might have to take out a mortgage of $140,000. (The gold and silver I had inherited was long gone by this point.) Wells, however, thought we should hold the mortgage to $100,000. After pondering this problem, I decided that it might be all right to take out the larger mortgage because we did have a tremendous value in the Estes property that we could probably use as back up. That's why it occurred to me to check in with the Dreiss family.

Wells and I had been very close friends with our Estes Park neighbors, Bill and Jackie Dreiss, for over twenty years, ever since they built a cabin about a quarter of a mile from ours. They were wonderful people who loved the mountains as much as we did, and we shared many pleasant meals together. On a couple of occasions when we visited San Antonio, we had been entertained in their Texas ranch home, and they had visited us once in Maine. We had also often seen their son Tom, his wife Annette, and their two children when they came to spend their vacations at the cabin. Now, the Dreiss's cabin was only about twenty-five feet from the line of our 45-acre lot, so we owned their backyard. It was hardly surprising that Bill would from time to time remind us that they would love to buy a small piece of our land.

When I was trying to figure out the financing for our new house, Bill Dreiss was no longer alive, so I decided to call his son Tom. I explained to him that Wells and I would have to take out a larger mortgage than we had hoped in order to build our retirement house. I mentioned that we could feel that we weren't taking too much of a risk if we knew that he would still be interested in buying a piece of our 45-acre lot if we ever had trouble making our mortgage payments. Tom assured me that they were indeed still interested in buying any land we wanted to sell. He also suggested we consider just selling them a piece of land right away so we wouldn't have to take out a mortgage and would have some extra money to enjoy traveling in our retirement. At this time, Tom and Annette were looking ahead and thinking that within another decade there would be seven families sharing their present cabin. They wanted some day to build their own cabin nearby so they could spend longer periods at Estes.

The more I thought about it, the more it seemed like a good idea to sell Tom some land at this time, so I sent an e-mail to Mark on August 13, 2002, that contained the following passages:

Last night Tom suggested that he would very much like to buy the whole forty acres [*we later learned that this lot was actually 45 acres*], build just one cabin (rustic style), and put easements on all the rest of the land so that it could never be developed further. In the course of the conversation, when I was expressing my concern that Diane's share of the forty acres could fall into the hands of a developer when she died, Tom pointed out that anyone inheriting that land from her would have the right to use our road to access it. That is of course a terrifying thought. (Tom's land abuts the forty acres, so he would not need our road access.)· . . .

One other option that occurred to me is that Wells and I could hold back ten of our twenty acres, and we could sell Tom thirty—ten from you, ten from Diane, and ten from us. That way we could keep open the option of the girls building there some day. . . . I think it's possible that we could get almost as much money from Tom for 30 acres as for 40 as long as we all agreed on where the eventual homesites that were allowed in the easements would go. [*I mentioned that I thought we might be able to get $500,000 from Tom, which would have been $166,000 each for Mark and Diane and $166,000 for the quarter share Wells and I would retain.*] . . . . I'm very much afraid that if we don't give these issues careful thought we could end up forever regretting the fact that we didn't sacrifice at least part of the forty acres to ensure the viability of the main property.

The careful analyses of various important issues that I e-mailed Mark almost always elicited only a one- or two-sentence reply. His reply to my August 13 e-mail was, "There is absolutely no way I would sell any part whatsoever of Estes Park to anyone." It was most frustrating that he would not even comment on how he thought we could protect ourselves from the possibility of Diane carrying out her threat to leave her share of the property outside the family and wasn't willing to discuss these issues by telephone.

As the result of Mark's emphatic "no," Wells and I had a meeting in August of 2002 with an estate planning lawyer in Boulder named Andrew Cunningham. He advised us that given two unusual circumstances, it made sense for me to carry out an undisclosed sale of my one-quarter undivided share of the 45 acres that I owned as a tenant in common with Wells, Diane, and Mark. These were the two unusual circumstances: (1) Tom Dreiss didn't want to build a cabin for another ten years and (2) Mark, who hadn't set foot on the property in thirteen years, was adamantly opposed to anyone selling any of the 105 acres our family owned or building any other cabins on it. He was extremely obese, had an unhealthy lifestyle, and had high blood pressure, so I thought it was quite possible that he would not live long enough to know I had sold my share of the land.

Mark in fact died on September 17, 2005. If the family had trusted my judgment or at least conceded that it was my decision to make as the owner of a quarter share of the 45 acres, my marriage would be intact and very serious damage to my relationships with my older daughters, Marie and Kathryn, would not have occurred. Unfortunately, the events set in motion in the summer of 2002 led to a long series of "eleventh hour" episodes.

On March 1, 2004, after trying a couple of times to talk to Mark in person, I left a message on his voice mail saying that I had just been told by a Denver lawyer that if Diane, then sixty-seven, carried out her oft-repeated threat to leave her share of Estes outside the family, then chances were considerably over fifty percent that we would lose the entire property shortly after her death. (Later I learned from another lawyer that the chances of losing the property would have been closer to ninety percent.) I told Mark I would like to meet with him in Vancouver, Brunswick, or anywhere else to discuss what we could do to protect the property. He e-mailed me back to say he was busy, so personal meetings were not an option. He did not suggest that we discuss these crucial issues by phone or e-mail. Instead, on March 3 Mark attempted to call my daughter Kathryn, who was a lawyer in Colorado. She was out jogging when he called, so her husband Steve took a brief message.

As a result of Mark's call, Kathryn called me up and shouted at me hysterically for a long time just because I had called my brother without her permission. In the course of the conversation, she told me that if I kept doing things like this, it would ruin our relationship, a statement that I found extremely upsetting. When she was haranguing me, Kathryn didn't have much of an idea what I had said to Mark in the message I had left on his voice mail. This made her extreme reaction even more out-of-line. She was so upset that she went in to work a couple of hours late. Steve e-mailed everyone in the family that he was so concerned at how upset she was that he wanted to suggest a moratorium of a week on any further discussion of these issues. They were expecting their first child in September, and he said that he feared that this dispute could have an effect on Kathryn's pregnancy.

The moratorium lasted until April 11, when Kathryn said to me during a phone call in which Wells and Steve were also taking part: "If you take unilateral action, if you act behind our backs, it will ruin our relationship." (I take notes on important phone conversations.) I started to sob and to have heart palpitations and chest pain when she made that threat and then Steve underlined the threat by saying, "Get it through your head, Alison, if you don't take unilateral action it won't ruin the relationship." I was sobbing because I would have hoped that Kathryn's love for me was unconditional, not something I could lose if I sold a piece of land over her objections. To me, that love was virtually already gone if she thought she could put that kind of condition on it. I later learned that the family considered my sobbing and heart irregularity to be a sign of mental illness.

Despite this upsetting phone call and the strong opposition I was encountering from Marie and Kathryn and their spouses, I continued to give very serious consideration to the matter of selling some land to Tom Dreiss. It was, after all, my decision to make; it was my land, not my children's, although it was clear they thought differently. Marie had a Harvard law degree, Kathryn a Yale law degree, and their husbands, Dino and Steve, both had Ph.D.s from Harvard. This may have been one reason why they were convinced they should be "running the show," not their sixty-six-year-old mother.

Unfortunately, my attempts to discuss the land issue with Wells always went nowhere because he would just say something like, "We shouldn't sell any of the Estes land unless we're forced to do so" or "We shouldn't consider selling land to Tom because it's upsetting the children so much." I finally decided that given the complexity of the issue, it made sense for all concerned for me to put together a position paper considering all the possible outcomes if Diane left her share of Estes outside the family. I hoped that although Wells was always dismissive of my attempts to discuss the issue, he might read my analysis and tell me where he agreed or disagreed. So it was that on May 27, 2004, I presented to Wells a six-page "white paper" that I had put together over the preceding few weeks to analyze why I thought we should sell part of the 45 acres to Tom Dreiss.

My analysis presented my "guesstimates" of the land values, which totaled $5.5 million. (A report by a Denver appraiser I later hired found a total value of one million less.) I noted that Diane and I each owned an Estes share worth $1.8 million. My white paper contained an analysis of why it would be almost impossible for us to save the property if Diane were to die and leave her share outside the family. One scenario was covered by the following passage:

> 3. Johnsons or Johnsons and Mark together try to take out a mortgage to cover $1.8 million. An Estes bank told me that on a loan for land purchase like this, a down payment of 25 percent would be required. That would be $450,000 for the down payment. At an interest rate of 7 percent, the interest on the balance of $1,340,000 in the first year would be $94,500, and one would be adding to that some payment on the principal. These sums are obviously way out in the stratosphere for our family.

Underlying the analysis in my white paper was the knowledge I had recently acquired that Tom Dreiss had way more money than I had realized. (He always maintained a very low profile in our hillside community in Estes.) He was clearly a multimillionaire, so I realized that working with him would give our family the best chance to keep almost all of our land pristine because he was willing to put conservation easements on almost all the land he might acquire from us. The white paper included this passage under the heading: "Advantages of Selling Tom Part of My Ten-Acre Share of the Forty Acres":

1. We lock Tom once and for all into the forty acres so that he will always be waiting in the wings to buy any amount of Diane's share necessary to protect Estes. Tom has told me that he is "always looking for land." Last year Annette and he looked at a couple of large lots on the Devil's Gulch Road. This year they also looked at some land that was very attractive, although it didn't have the great views our forty acres has. If I don't sell Tom some land soon, we run the huge risk that he will buy elsewhere. He can see that good cabin sites are rapidly disappearing in the area. He is also well aware of the danger that the Deans' land [*160 acres adjacent to our 45 acres*] will soon be developed. At this point, he is willing to live with that possibility. I think there's a chance that if that possibility became a reality, with several houses on the south part of the southern meadow, Tom might think twice about whether he wants to build next to those houses.

If we some day had to sell part of the forty acres to someone else, they will be driving by our cabin to access their land. Tom is an incredible, irreplaceable asset for us. We are tremendously lucky to have someone who has a large amount of capital available, wants very much to help us preserve the land, can access his site or sites without driving by our cabin, can help provide road, water, and electricity access if one of the girls build up there, and will be a wonderful neighbor.

The white paper also contained an important section about my desire to obtain a reserve fund that could be used to pay for some very serious health problems our youngest daughter Christine had developed, problems that were key to the land dispute. All three of my daughters and I had developed at various points in our lives a condition known as multiple chemical sensitivity (MCS).[1] People who develop MCS become very reactive to everyday chemical exposures such as those associated with paint, new carpet, perfume, air fresheners, cleaning products, cigarette smoke, gasoline, and traffic fumes. This sensitivity can make it enormously difficult for them to find places to live and work where they will not develop symptoms like migraines or joint pain or asthma attacks.

Christine's chemical sensitivity problems were so severe that she was unable to attend school or to work from the age of sixteen until she was twenty-one. On a very sad and rainy night, I helped her carry all her belongings down four flights of stairs from her dorm room at Exeter. Christine had loved the school, and we were both feeling devastated that her health problems were forcing her to leave. As I was starting the car to drive back to Maine, I said to her, "Christine, somewhere out there, there is health and happiness for you, and I will help you find them."

That was a taller order than I realized. Over the next three years, I took Christine all over the country and even to Germany for four weeks in search of any treatment that might restore her health.[2] We even lived

---

[1] Information about multiple chemical sensitivity is available on the website of the Chemical Sensitivity Foundation, which I founded in 2001, www.chemicalsensitivityfoundation.org. See my personal website, www.alisonjohnsonmcs.com, for information about the books I have written and the documentaries I have produced/directed on the subject of MCS, including my 2006 documentary, *The Toxic Clouds of 9/11: A Looming Health Disaster*, which I showed on Capitol Hill. In its March 1, 2007, issue *Library Journal* had this to say about the film: "raise[s] extremely troubling issues of which many individuals are unaware. . . . well produced and soundly researched, with highly knowledgeable experts offering commentary. *Toxic Clouds . . .* resonates so deeply in the public psyche; it belongs in every public library."

[2] The silver lining to this cloud was that as a result of our travels in search of a "cure" for multiple chemical sensitivity, I eventually compiled a statistical survey of 351 people with MCS showing how they reacted to 160 different therapies, many of them alternative. This survey has saved many chemically sensitive people from wasting their money on treatments that are unlikely to help and in some cases could make them worse.

in Fort Collins, Colorado, for two years to see if a climate with less mold would improve her health. Finally, we just settled down in Maine and reduced Christine's chemical exposures as best we could. After a couple of years, she was able to take some classes at Bowdoin College, just a couple of blocks from our house. The next year she entered a top university, where she received her master's degree and is currently finishing her Ph.D. thesis in economics while working in another city. All this was possible, however, only by ensuring that she had an apartment without a gas stove or new carpet or pesticide applications. Dorm rooms or shared apartments with roommates using scented products were not an option. Over the years, Wells and I had spent a very large amount of money on all the things we had done to try to get Christine well and through college and grad school. We also had to pay full tuition at expensive universities for two of our daughters because my Estes property precluded them from getting scholarships.

By 2004, Wells and I found ourselves in a situation in which we were carrying a mortgage of $140,000 on our new retirement home and had no savings accounts and owned no Treasury Bills. We were also putting out $15,000 a year for Christine's apartment while she was working on her Ph.D., and I was very concerned about how we could support her if chemical exposures made her unable to work for a prolonged period. By this point, I was all too aware through my work that large numbers of chemically sensitive people have had to drop out of the workforce because of their inability to find a workplace they can tolerate.

As a result of these concerns, my white paper about selling the land also included this section:

2. I get money to set up a trust fund for Christine. This is something I very much want to do. Christine has been dealt a lousy genetic hand, and I want to know as I approach the end of my life that I have done everything possible to make her life a little less difficult. There are almost certainly going to be future episodes of serious problems, and when that happens, I want Christine to know that she has the funds to get her through an extended period when she can't work. . . .

I've always had in the back of my mind that part of Estes could be sold to cover expenses that might arise for Christine, but it's increasingly clear to me that it's up to me to take that action now. Otherwise, I can envision that some day there will be arguments about whether it's necessary to sell some of the land for various of Christine's needs.

My disappointment was great when Wells's only response to my white paper was to say that it was "just a bunch of hypotheticals." When I suggested that we try to pin down some of the land values and financial issues involved by having the land appraised and consulting financial planners, he rejected my suggestion, saying there was no reason to spend that money because we shouldn't sell the land. He didn't even bother to discuss the many points I had raised in my white paper.

My white paper had not convinced Wells that I should sell a piece of land, but it convinced me that I should move ahead, so I arranged to meet Tom in Estes to walk the 45 acres. This meeting was difficult to set up for various reasons. That summer I had planned to stay in Maine for the first part of June to enjoy my garden, but Wells had headed to Estes as soon as he finished teaching. Tom and I decided that the only mutually convenient time to walk the land was the weekend of June 11-12. As it turned out, Kathryn and Steve were planning to spend that weekend with Wells at the cabin, which complicated matters greatly. With Kathryn six months pregnant, I didn't want to provoke another hysterical episode of the kind that Steve had considered so dangerous in March. I also knew that it would be impossible for me to walk the land with Tom and enter into preliminary negotiations about price if Kathryn was doing everything she could to stop matters from going forward. I had not been Kathryn's mother for over thirty years without realizing that she had a will of iron. If you crossed her, she would go to unbelievable lengths to get her way.

In order to have a rational, unemotional conversation about the land with Tom, I decided to leave for Colorado earlier than I had intended and to stay for one night in a motel in Estes so that Tom and I could spend the weekend of June 11-12 exploring the 45 acres and discussing the options without Kathryn being aware of what we were doing.

By the end of Sunday afternoon, Tom and I were in agreement on a building site for him that would be close to his present cabin so that he could access it from his other land. Early that evening I called Wells at the cabin to ask if Kathryn and Steve had left yet. When he said they had already left, I told him that I was in Estes and had spent a night at a motel so that I could walk the land with Tom without Kathryn's interference. That evening I urged Wells to go up to the land with Tom and me the next morning so that he could see that the site we had chosen for Tom would not be readily visible from the site where someone in my family would be most likely to build. Wells refused to join us. He also refused to join me in consulting the Denver lawyer I was using, although I had told Wells that it appeared that Tom would pay me $400,000 for six acres, a sum of money that would have paid off our mortgage and given us a large reserve fund for Christine's future needs.

Things were relatively quiet for the next month. Then everything exploded in mid-July when I took Marie and Dino up the mountainside to see where Tom would like to build a cabin. As we were sitting there discussing the possibility, Marie suddenly said to me that if I carried out an undisclosed sale to Tom, "You will never see me again, you will never see Dino again, you will never see Kathryn again, you will never see Steve again, and you will never see your grandson." (This grandson who was about to be born may well be my only grandchild.) I felt as if Marie had kicked me in the stomach. She then said that I didn't need to worry about having money for Christine's future needs because if Christine ever needed money, Kathryn and she would take care of her. I replied that I didn't see how I could rely on that statement since Marie had not worked in five years and Dino and she were living in a tiny apartment that was only 350 square feet and also served as his office. Her response was that Dino's business was going well, so they would have the money to help Christine. I was not convinced. Businesses can falter, people can die, people can get divorced. I wanted a sure thing for Christine.

The other shoe dropped with a sickening thud on July 25, when Kathryn's husband, Steve, who had spent perhaps thirty days on the property compared to the sixty summers I had spent there, sent me a very rude e-mail signed "Steve (and Kathryn)." This e-mail stated that my plans to sell the land had "taken on the appearance of a runaway train heading over a cliff" and ended with the words: "If four of your friends tell you you are drunk, you should give them your car keys and lie down." That e-mail, which I received late that night at the cabin, was a devastating blow, one of the worst things that has ever happened to me. With a few strokes at the keyboard, Steve had gone far to end my enjoyment of a beautiful property that had meant the world to me for sixty summers. It was hard to sleep that night because it was so clear to me that in the future my older daughters and their spouses were going to marginalize me at Estes as the elderly parent they would barely tolerate.

As the result of Steve's harsh e-mail, I decided to abandon the option of an undisclosed sale. Instead I notified Mark and Diane that I wanted to rearrange the ownership of our five parcels of land so that I could build a separate cabin and also sell some of the 45 acres to Tom. I came to that momentous decision because the recent family events had made it all too clear that it would no longer be relaxing or pleasant to share the main cabin with Marie, Kathryn, Steve, and Dino. I was also heartsick that my brother and sister's impossible eccentricities and personalities had set in motion a chain of events that had had a disastrous effect on my relationships with Marie, Kathryn, and their spouses. At this point, I had had it with Mark and Diane and wanted to reduce further property entanglement with them as much as I could.

August passed, however, with no real response from Mark to my proposal, except for a couple of brief e-mails that didn't really address the issue. Realizing that my attempts at e-mail communication were going nowhere, on September 16, 2004, I called him to discuss my proposal for rearranging ownership of our lots so that I could build myself a small cabin where I could live in peace and sell some land to Tom, which would help pay for my new cabin and provide a nest egg for Christine's future needs. Unfortunately, Mark was totally unsympathetic with my desire to raise money for Christine's future. He emphatically said he would never sign papers dividing up the 45 acres so that I could sell 6 acres from my 11-acre share to Tom. He kept urging me to see a counselor. Mark's comments about my seeing a counselor and impressions I was getting from other family members made me fear that if I did not sell the land soon they might in some way try to stop me on the grounds that I was mentally ill. I was not mentally ill. I had never been depressed, had never consulted a psychiatrist or counselor, and had always been a center of stability in both my families.

Faced with this very difficult situation, I decided to sell my entire quarter undivided share (11 acres) of the 45 acres to Tom before family members could try to stop me because I didn't need anyone's cooperation to do that. I signed a buy/sell agreement with Tom in late

September but did not announce that fact to Wells and the girls until it was a fait accompli to ensure they didn't try to have me declared incompetent in order to stop the sale. My fears that the family might try to take action against me on the grounds that I was mentally ill were hardly based on paranoia. I knew that in early August Wells had made what was supposed to be a secret phone call to Tom in which he tried to discourage him from moving forward to purchase the land. In October, I learned from Tom that Wells had made statements to him about my mental condition in that August phone call. Two years later I at last obtained proof that Wells was questioning my mental state in legal documents when I received copies of papers filed with a Colorado court in 2006. In these documents, Wells stated that he had told Tom during that secret August 2004 phone call that "as a result of Alison Johnson's actions, he and his family were very concerned about Alison Johnson's mental condition." Wells's message to Tom in that phone call was clearly, "Don't buy the land from Alison." Legal and financial advisers later commented that they were amazed that I had found someone who wanted the land so badly that he would give me between two and four times its market value, depending on the appraisal. With that one secret phone call, Wells could have ruined my chance for a sale that would ensure Christine's future with far more money than I could have obtained from another purchaser.

My perilous situation in the fall of 2004 became even clearer on October 31, when Wells handed me a letter that he also sent to me officially via a Denver lawyer about a month later. In this letter, Wells referred to his "serious and growing concerns about your mental stability" and stated: "What has become abundantly clear over recent months is that you are suffering from some kind of mental illness and that you need treatment by a psychiatrist. . . . Given the history of your family . . . it would not be surprising to see some form of mental illness manifesting itself in you as well. . . . Intervention and proper treatment can prevent further deterioration in your condition ."

I read Wells's words in a state of shock. He had been married to me for forty years and knew that I was very stable mentally. In fact, that morning when he handed me the letter referring to "the history of your family," which was of course a reference to my mother's manic-depression, or bipolar illness, he commented that he had never seen me depressed. At any rate, the letter made it abundantly evident that I was facing the frightening possibility that the family might move against me to try to reverse the land sale. I was painfully aware of my vulnerability with five family members all saying I was mentally ill—Wells with his MIT Ph.D., Marie with her Harvard law degree, Kathryn with her Yale law degree, and Dino and Steve with their Harvard Ph.D.s. Would I be believed in the face of the five of them?

The timing seemed particularly ironic when Wells handed me his letter saying I was so mentally ill that I couldn't be trusted to handle business affairs. I had in the preceding two weeks been to Texas to film Ross Perot and the former head of Walter Reed Army Medical Center because I wanted to include some new footage in a revised edition of my documentary *Gulf War Syndrome: Aftermath of a Toxic Battlefield*. The night before Wells handed me the letter, I had just returned from a conference at Hilton Head at which the American Academy of Environmental Medicine had given me its Carleton Lee Award for "exemplary efforts in furthering the principles of environmental medicine." It was a startling juxtaposition of one of the best moments in my life with one of the worst.

As these alarming events were unfolding in the fall of 2004, I started telling some of my close friends and cousins what was going on. They were appalled that the family was saying I was mentally ill. I'm sure that many of them thought that my family members didn't really believe that but were just using this charge to stop the land sale. It's clear to me, however, that in what amounted to a *folie à cinq* (a delusion shared by five), they had all convinced each other that I was mentally ill because they wanted so desperately to keep Tom from getting the land. It was also clear to me that they would never back off from this assertion because to admit they had been wrong would be to admit that they had done something terrible to me.

Given the danger of my situation, I decided to move quickly to assemble evidence that my land sale was a reasonable decision. I arranged for an Estes Park appraiser to meet me on our property in mid-November so that we could walk the land before snow drifts made it inaccessible. Of course, it was rather unusual to have the land appraised after it had already been sold, but Wells had not been willing to spend the money for an appraisal when I suggested it in May. Now that I had received from Tom the first installment on the land sale, I had my own bank account and could pay for the appraisal.

I didn't alert Wells that I was leaving for Colorado until the very last minute so that he wouldn't have time to try to organize a way to stop me from leaving. From the airport in Boston, I called Kathryn, who lives in Boulder, to ask if I could visit my new grandson the next morning. Fortunately, she gave me permission to do so, perhaps because I caught her off guard. I did have a wonderful time holding my three-month-old grandson in my arms. Little did I realize that I would not be allowed to hold him in my arms again for almost a year and a half.

Fortunately, there was no early snowstorm, so I was able to walk the Estes property with the appraiser. He agreed that the 45 acres was a gorgeous piece of property but also said it had huge problems with accessibility and road and water costs. I later learned that another important factor reducing the value of that land was that local insurance companies had stopped writing fire insurance policies for cabins in remote locations that could not be reached by a fire truck.

While I was in Boulder, I met twice with Andrew Cunningham, the lawyer who had two years earlier discussed with Wells and me the possibility of my selling my undivided quarter share of the 45 acres to Tom Dreiss. I asked Kathryn to join us for the second meeting. During that second conversation, Andrew said that given the enormously complex and unusual situation, there had always been much to be said for my transacting an undisclosed sale to Tom Dreiss. He thought that Mark's refusal in his March 5, 2004, e-mail to pursue my plea to meet with him personally to discuss how we might try to protect Estes from being lost by Diane's leaving her share outside the family was all the more reason why I could not be faulted for having pursued an undisclosed sale.

In the course of the meeting, Kathryn told Andrew that my making the trip to Colorado and spending money on an appraisal, as well as not telling Wells in advance, were all signs of mental illness. When Kathryn stated that Marie and she thought I was manic-depressive like my mother, I asked her point blank if they were contemplating taking legal action to reverse the sale of the land by questioning my mental competence. She refused in front of Andrew to say that the family wasn't going to question my competency in court. During the next two years, I kept trying to get Wells to say that they weren't going to try that, but he would always dismiss my entreaties with a comment like, "I'm not going to give away my legal strategy." I didn't get the proof of their intentions, however, until I obtained those relevant court documents in the fall of 2006.

When Andrew Cunningham asked Kathryn whether she objected only to the undisclosed aspect of the proposed sale or was opposed to the sale period, she indicated that she was opposed to it period. He then asked her what her plan had been for handling all these complex issues. She offered none. At one point, Andrew made a crucial statement with regard to my sale to Tom, "It's the most rational thing I can imagine." Since I sold the land for between two and four times its value according to the two appraisals I later received, few people would consider the sale an irrational act.

After Kathryn left our meeting with Andrew Cunningham, I stayed to talk to him for a few more minutes. One of his first comments was, "You certainly have a lot of negative energy coming your direction." (Kathryn had been highly emotional during the meeting, with her anger toward me readily apparent.) Andrew made another telling comment that was particularly interesting, given his decades of experience as an estate lawyer. "I've dealt with a lot of families in my time," he told me, "but I've never seen a family dynamic like yours before."

A couple of weeks later I had yet another indication that the family was trying to shoehorn me into a manic-depressive diagnosis. On the day before Thanksgiving, I happened to mention to Wells that I wanted to put a spot light on the Christmas wreath on the garage that year, and I asked him what I needed to buy to set up the spot light. "Alison," he said, "this is manic. It's not even Thanksgiving." I responded angrily that his comment was outrageous. I wasn't putting up decorations the day before Thanksgiving; I was just making plans for what I needed to purchase.

Devastating news arrived on December 3, when Kathryn sent me an e-mail announcing that she was bringing the baby to the East Coast on December 18 to see all the relatives but I was to be excluded. She said, "It wouldn't be healthy for me to spend time with you now." I e-mailed her to suggest that since she didn't want to spend time with me, she could leave the baby with Wells and Christine in Christine's Cambridge apartment while she went for a walk for a half hour, or even just fifteen minutes, so that I could see him briefly. She refused to agree, and it was a very sad day when I saw Wells drive off without me to see Kathryn and the baby. Marie and Dino also didn't come home for Christmas that year for the first time. I couldn't help thinking how very odd it was that Marie and Kathryn were saying they thought I was manic-depressive but were treating me very badly, while Diane and I had always done everything we could for Mom when she developed mental problems. Within the next couple of months, I became worried enough that the family would try to have me declared mentally ill and incompetent to have sold the land that I sought counsel from a Boston lawyer who specializes in cases in which family members try to seize control of a relative's property on the grounds of mental incompetence. He arranged for me to meet with Dr. Charles Welch, a practicing psychiatrist at Massachusetts General Hospital and a Harvard Medical School professor who is also a former president of the Massachusetts Medical Society. I spent almost three hours with Dr. Welch and presented him with all the e-mails and letters and other documentation indicating that family members had come up with this charge in order to reverse the land sale. At the end of the afternoon, he said that I was not mentally ill and that the whole idea was "ludicrous." The conclusion of Dr. Welch's official report, produced after three additional meetings with me, stated: "I find that Alison Johnson does not suffer from any mental illness. Specifically, I find no evidence of depression, mania, hypomania, or psychosis. . . . I also find her to have exceptional intellectual capacity, especially with regard to her analytic skills."

When I returned from my first meeting with Dr. Welch, I announced to Wells that I had consulted an eminent Boston psychiatrist and he had said I was not mentally ill. Wells was not at all happy to hear that news and said that Dr. Welch didn't understand the situation because he hadn't talked to other family members. I was of course dismayed that Wells didn't want to give up the idea that I was mentally ill. I was not totally surprised, however, because I realized that Wells in effect "wanted" me to be mentally ill so that he could reverse my land sale to Tom. For several months, my Boston lawyer and I tried to get Wells to meet with Dr. Welch and me, but Wells said he would only meet with Dr. Welch if he could do so privately. Dr. Welch would not agree to this.

On May 20, Wells responded to a "fish-or-cut bait" e-mail from Steve Howard, my Boston lawyer, by officially declining to meet with Dr. Welch and me. That evening I initiated a crucial conversation with Wells in which I said something like, "I'm not going to stay married to you forever if you can't give up the idea that I'm mentally ill. . . . . This could lead to divorce." I told Wells that his refusal to meet with Dr. Welch and me led me to doubt that he would ever give up the idea that I was mentally ill. Unfortunately, by now it was obvious to me that Wells was dead set on using charges that I was mentally ill to reverse my land sale and thought he would be in a better position to do so if he could assert that Dr. Welch had formed an opinion without any input from my family. When I brought up the subject of divorce that evening, about the only response Wells offered was to say the idea of divorce was ridiculous and was just another sign of my mental illness. Wells didn't bring up the subject of divorce during the next sixteen days before he left for Colorado on June 6, which seemed most strange.

I gave up going to Colorado that summer because of a letter that Wells's Denver lawyer sent to Steve Howard on May 27. This letter stated that the family wanted me to undergo a psychiatric evaluation by someone besides Dr. Welch and laid out a fairly detailed formula that included private meetings between the evaluating psychiatrist and each family member. I feared that there was some chance that the family might go to the incredible length of trying to have me hospitalized in a psychiatric facility in Colorado to obtain an evaluation. The Denver lawyer who had handled the land sale for me did not consider these fears unfounded. He said that the letter from Wells's Denver lawyer could be viewed as laying the ground work for such a hospitalization. He also learned in a conversation with Wells's lawyer that the family thought that my mental health was "deteriorating" and that I was becoming "increasingly irrational."

In a leading book in the field of mental health, *Overcoming Depression* (rev. ed.), psychiatrist Demitri Papolos and coauthor Janice Papolos note that many states have recently amended their laws to make involuntary commitment easier:

> Addressing the issue, the American Psychiatric Association has devised a model commitment law that would allow commitments not only when patients are dangerous to self and others, but also *when the patients are suffering and would be likely to deteriorate without treatment*; in the presence of a major psychiatric illness that could be treated, provided that treatment

is available; and when patients are mentally incapable of deciding for themselves. (pp. 273-74, italics added)

I found it troubling that Wells's four-page letter of October 31, 2004, contained language that could be viewed as establishing a basis for the italicized conditions above. Later I learned that Marie and Kathryn had helped draft his letter, which contained these phrases: "What has become abundantly clear over recent months is that you are *suffering* from some kind of mental illness" . . . "Intervention and proper treatment can prevent further *deterioration* in your condition " (italics added). Perhaps the desire to make these statements in a legal context was the reason for the very odd fact that Wells didn't just give me that October 31 letter, but also had his Denver lawyer send it to me.

I finally concluded that spending the summer with Wells at the cabin in Estes, with Marie and Dino there for the month of July and Kathryn and Steve only an hour away in Boulder, would mean that I would be greatly outnumbered if they did try to force me into a psychiatric hospital for an evaluation. To add to the risk, Kathryn was very well connected in the Colorado legal profession. It didn't sound like a relaxing vacation, so I decided to spend a more peaceful summer in Maine.

On a couple of occasions in June, I called Wells to see how things were going at the cabin. Then on July 10, I sent him a letter in which I told him I was starting divorce proceedings and offered this explanation:

This mailing is of course a follow-up to my statement to you on May 20 that I would not stay married to you forever if you were not able to give up the idea that I am mentally ill. It is obvious to me that you will not even begin to give up that idea while the battle over the partition of the 45 acres continues, and that battle may take a year or more to resolve. Your failure between May 20 and your June 6 departure to bring up the subject of my raising of the divorce possibility and your failure to call during the month you have been in Estes make it quite clear that you are not going to give up the idea that I am mentally ill. I have reached a point in life where I want to put all of this behind me after a very difficult year and move forward independently.

On July 26, Wells called me from Estes for the first time since he had left Maine seven weeks earlier. (My Boston lawyer noted the irony that Wells was contending that I was mentally ill and didn't even call for seven weeks to see how I was doing.) Wells started the call that day by saying: "I miss you a lot. The cabin doesn't seem right without you; it's so identified with you. I wish you were here." I replied that I might have been able to come if he and Marie and Kathryn had been willing to sign a statement saying they wouldn't try to force me into a psychiatric hospital for evaluation while I was there. Wells replied that they could not sign such a statement.

I found it particularly disturbing that during this period Kathryn and Marie made phone calls to try to undermine my position with a friend and a cousin who had been very supportive of me. When Kathryn called my cousin Linda, she told Linda that the fact that I wanted to divorce Wells was a sign of mental illness. Linda rejoined that she had just spent time with me in Lincoln with our old family friend from Palisade, Helen Brown, and her daughter, Shirley, and that I had seemed fine and we all had a great time together. Kathryn replied, "That's part of the illness—high energy and very sociable." (Linda took notes and I took notes.) Now, the four of us had spent a wonderful two or three hours that afternoon reminiscing and laughing about old times in Palisade. If I was manic, so were Helen, Shirley, and Linda.

Marie in turn made a phone call to the daughter of my closest Brunswick friend, who had known me for over forty years, in an attempt to get the daughter to tell her mother to back off in her support of me. Fortunately, I could unwind that one by sending the daughter the report from Dr. Welch saying that I was not suffering from any mental illness.

These phone calls that my older daughters were making left me feeling very uneasy. I happened to find out about these two calls, and I also heard that Wells had raised issues about my mental stability with an Estes neighbor. I was left wondering how many other people had been told that I was mentally ill.

In late August 2006, I learned of yet another instance in which one of my daughters was making entirely inaccurate statements about me to people outside the family. Tom Dreiss called me to report a conversation that Marie had had with his brother Dick at our annual homeowners association picnic in Estes Park. She had made one statement that was so bizarre that I called up Dick to hear it from him firsthand, and I wrote down exactly what he said as he was talking. He told me that Marie had said, "Mom was like a high school girl in love with the high school quarterback, so in love with Tom she lost sight of reality." Clearly, I was not the one who had lost sight of reality.

After almost four years of wondering what Wells or Marie and Kathryn have said to whom, I've reached a point in life where I believe it is important for me to tell my story while I am still alive and well. In the fall of 2006, I had a small stroke with no apparent symptoms except for a slight loss of peripheral vision that my optometrist noted. An MRI did show that I had recently had a stroke. At any rate, a person who has had a stroke has a thirty percent chance of having another one in the next five or six years. That's one more reason I decided to tell my story while I am able to do so.

A year ago I moved into a new house I had built in a beautiful Maine retirement community called Highland Green that is located across the river from Brunswick. My backyard connects directly to a 230-acre nature preserve where I can hike or cross-country ski. The community is ideal for my chemical sensitivity because there is no wood smoke and very low pesticide use. This move also made sense because I can still see all my old friends in the area and make many additional ones in my new community, which offers a very active social life among people who have moved here from all over the country. I felt that I could make a fresh start at Highland Green, whereas in the Brunswick community I was likely to be viewed as the woman who had divorced that nice Bowdoin professor after forty-two years of marriage.

That hope for a fresh start was something of an illusion, as I learned during the recent holiday season, because our worlds can interconnect in unsuspected ways. I discovered that a man who lives in a nearby house has a brother-in-law who roomed with Wells at Amherst. I also learned that a woman who lives a block away has a daughter-in-law who is my daughter Kathryn's best friend from Maine.

Pondering the situation for a few weeks left me convinced that I didn't want to continue through life wondering who had heard what rumors about me. I realized that publishing this family memoir would provide ample evidence for the wisdom of my seizing the opportunity to sell a piece of land that would insure there was always money to handle any health problems that might arise for my youngest daughter. During the conflict of the last four years, my family has continually complained about my "doomsday scenarios." Readers of this family memoir will see that life in my family was indeed an unremitting series of doomsday scenarios playing out.

I also realized that by including an Epilogue I could lay out the facts concerning the family's mistaken allegations that I am bipolar. Of course, I regret that I have had to relate things that they have done and said that they will be embarrassed to see made public. In other parts of their lives, they have done many good things for others, but as many of my friends have said, their treatment of me has been appalling. I am writing this Epilogue because I believe that their desire for privacy is trumped by my right not to be considered mentally ill when this is not the case. Should women who are beat up by their husbands conceal that fact from others because it will make their husbands look bad? There was no physical violence in my case, but the emotional violence has been extreme.

This is not a decision I have made lightly. When I was debating the land sale, I sought the counsel of a couple of close friends. As I was contemplating publishing my family memoir with this added Epilogue, I again consulted a few close friends, and they encouraged me to publish it. One friend said, "You've been a punching bag for too long. It's time you punched back."

*   *   *   *

In yet another Krotter family "eleventh hour" event, my brother Mark died on September 17, 2005, leaving a will that dismayed the family. (Incidentally, Mark made this will on May 14, 2004, over two months before I announced to him that I was going to sell a piece of land to Tom Dreiss. I learned from two of his friends that he had been thinking along these lines for a few years.) At any rate, Diane, my three daughters, and I each received a token bequest of $1,000. He left his quarter undivided share of all five of our Estes lots to Rocky Mountain National Park "for use and conservation only as natural parkland." He also stated that if RMNP did not accept the bequest, his Estes property should go to Roosevelt National Forest for the same purpose.

It is hardly surprising that both Rocky Mountain National Park and Roosevelt National Forest turned down this bequest of an undivided share of land. According to Mark's will, the Colorado property should be passing to Margaret Yates, who divorced him in 1980, because she is the residual heir. Various people in my family are now engaged in legal maneuvering to try to keep that from happening. In the ultimate irony of the land battle, the next residual heir after Margaret is the Canadian Quakers, who are enjoined in the will to use the residual estate "for the sole purpose of opposing military conscription." If Margaret had not been alive, then once Rocky Mountain National Park and Roosevelt National Forest had declined the bequest, it would have passed to the Canadian Quakers. The Quakers would have had no choice according to the terms of the will but to cash out their share. That would have led to a significant amount, if not all, of our Estes property becoming a large development, exactly what Mark was trying so hard to prevent.

While the Estes Park issues relating to Mark's will were playing out at a maddeningly slow pace, our divorce was also not moving forward as fast as I had hoped. Wells and I were still sharing our house, one on each floor, with both of us using the kitchen. By this point, I had made the decision to build a much smaller house in Highland Green and wanted to move forward on construction so that I wouldn't have to share a house with Wells any longer than necessary. (As it was, we shared the house for almost two years after I announced my intention to divorce him.) Unfortunately, Wells did everything he could to prevent me from having this new house, including bringing a contempt of court action against me because I had paid a down payment on a lot before the divorce was settled. (I took advantage of an opportunity that suddenly arose to obtain a wonderful lot with unusual privacy and large areas for me to fill with shrubs and flowers.)

When it became clear that Wells was going to drag out the divorce proceedings as long as possible, which would have prevented me from holding onto this lot, I finally agreed to a divorce settlement under which I lost Estes in exchange for some cash up front and a series of installment payments. When $150,000 is subtracted off the total of these payments to correspond to my equity in our prior house, the $400,000 I will eventually receive is about thirty percent of the appraised value of my Estes property.

Wells gave me the supposed right to use the cabin in June for the rest of my life, but of course, he has no control over Diane and whoever ends up with Mark's share, so that clause is highly dubious. I had already stated to the family that I never wanted to go to Estes before the last two weeks of June because I wanted to be home in Maine when my lupine and other perennials bloom. In early 2007, I notified the family that I was going to attend an international seminar on Willa Cather in Paris and Avignon in late June and would like to spend three weeks in July and August in the small upper cabin, a very minimal place, some of which I built with my own hands. I received an e-mail from Kathryn signed by the rest of the family stating:

> Unfortunately, your request to come to the Estes property for three weeks in late July and early August this summer—instead of spending the month of June at the main cabin in accordance with the terms of the divorce settlement—doesn't fit in with our own plans for using the property during that period.

Kathryn did offer me the use of the main cabin for the last week in August and the first two or three weeks in September. Since the cabin is unheated and can become extremely cold in September, I passed on that option.

Needless to say, Kathryn's e-mail was a final blow because it was so clear that my family just didn't want me around. This rejection seemed particularly unfair when I had entertained Wells's mother for two weeks every summer from the time she was seventy-five until she was ninety-five and had also invited Dino's mother to spend a week with us one summer. And of course, over the years I had always invited Aunt Thelma to spend as long as she could with us every summer. I had managed the place in a manner to include relatives, not to exclude them.

But, after a period of grieving for my loss of Estes as one would grieve for the unexpected death of a beloved relative, I have moved on. I have established beautiful gardens around my house in Maine, and spending summers within a few miles of the Maine coast is hardly something to complain about. Of course, I miss the wonderful hikes I so enjoyed at Estes, but I have lined the entrance hall of my new home with beautiful photos of my favorite lakes and mountains. While I could still hike sixteen miles in June of 2006, it's only a matter of time until I could no longer climb those peaks anyway.

My life in my new house in a beautiful setting, with an active social life in a very pleasant retirement community, is a good one. My work as a writer and filmmaker has been rewarding and has kept me focused on positive and productive things during this difficult period of my life.

It seems appropriate to end this Epilogue by quoting from an e-mail that I sent to my family in April 2006:

Let me just try to say once more for the record (fruitless as it may be) something that none of you seem to get. This is an issue that I've wrestled with a great deal in the last year or so. The most basic part of me as a person is my belief in the integrity of my own mind, my belief that the thoughts that go through my head are rational. That is more basic than my role as a wife or mother. . . . My life would be meaningless if I were to buy into your theory that part of the thoughts going through my head are irrational because to me they are all rational (and many friends and professionals agree with me). Try to picture for a moment what it would be like to keep saying to yourself that your thoughts must be irrational because others say they are, despite the fact that they seem correct to you.

At any rate, my belief in the integrity of my mind is something that I value even more than I value the members of my family, and you will all just have to accept that. I have sacrificed myself for the family on many occasions, but this is one point on which I will not be moved.

These lines from the *Rubaiyat* of Omar Khayyam have been resonating in my mind for the past couple of years:

> The moving finger writes and having writ
> Moves on, nor all your piety and wit
> Shall lure it back to cancel half a line
> Nor all your tears wash out a word of it.